WOMEN
in
PRAISE
of the
SACRED

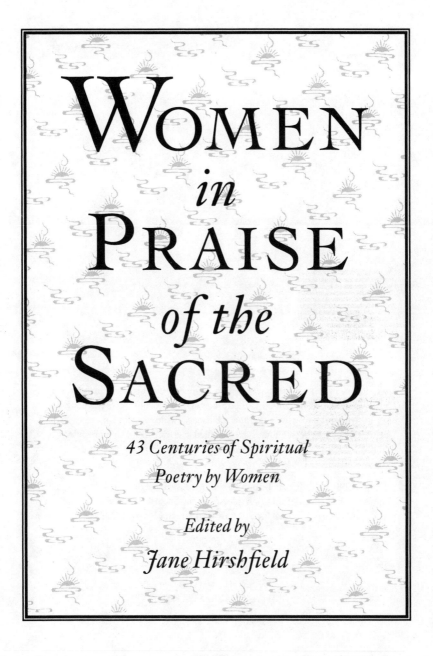

WOMEN
in
PRAISE
of the
SACRED

*43 Centuries of Spiritual
Poetry by Women*

Edited by

Jane Hirshfield

HarperCollins*Publishers*

HarperCollins books may be purchased for educational, business, or sales promotional use. For information please write: Special Markets Department, HarperCollins Publishers, Inc., 10 East 53rd Street, New York, NY 10022.

Copyright acknowledgments follow the index.

Designed by David Bullen
Typeset by Wilsted & Taylor

ISBN 0-06-016987-7

94   95   96   97   98   HC   10   9   8   7   6   5   4   3   2

For my teachers
and
For those whose voices have been lost

Contents

If they see
breasts and long hair coming
they call it woman,

if beard and whiskers
they call it man:

but, look, the self that hovers
in between
is neither man
nor woman

O Ramanatha

Devara Dasimayya
(tr. by A. K. Ramanujan)

Preface

Spiritual experience is fundamental to human life, and the profound connection that exists between each individual and a reality larger than the narrow or personal self (and yet fully resident within that self) is at the heart of every religious tradition. Still, the descriptions we have of this most intimate of encounters—the self meeting the Self—have come to us predominantly through the words of men. This is not because experience of the sacred is more common for men than for women, but because until quite recently social factors have for the most part encouraged men, and not women, to record their experience. This book—a record of intimacy with the sacred as it has been expressed by women in poetry, song, and prayer for over forty-three centuries—shows what common sense has always told us must be true: that the numinous does not discriminate, that infinitude and oneness do not exclude anyone.

While this collection is by no means comprehensive, it contains the work of women of many different cultures and traditions. There is poetry from ancient Sumeria; from classical Greece and Rome; from ancient Ethiopia, Israel, Iraq, and Byzantium; from India, Pakistan, China, Japan, Korea, and Vietnam; from Mexico and Chile and the United States; from Germany, the Netherlands, Italy, England, Wales, France, Spain, Finland, and Russia; and from several indigenous cultures. Some times and languages are better represented than others: there have been cultures where women were far more likely than others to be educated and to lead independent intellectual lives, and so far more likely as well to be able to give expression to their experience in a form that might last. There have also been times and places where spiritual life has been particularly alive for both men and women, and that too is reflected in the contents of this collection. Lastly, there have been cultures where the traditional poetry of the sacred is anonymous, or continues even now to be held in strict secrecy (the spiritual dream-songs of women aborigines in Australia, for example), and this has determined as well what the reader will find or not find in these pages.

Saying the Great Yes is the most basic gesture of the heart that has opened to beings and things, and so, as its title indicates, the spirituality of this book is a spirituality of affirmation. The pieces found here express the sacred as a living presence in human life—even in those poems that long for union or mourn its absence, their authors speak in the light of having experienced that which is now missing. Further, the idea of the "spiritual" in this book is not synonymous with "religious"; if anything, what is found in these pages is to a great extent the eccentric vision of the mystic and the peculiar speaking of the person who is following her own heart's language beyond the realm of the orthodox. Even so, several of the pieces included here have come to serve as foundation stones for entire literary traditions (most vividly, in the Judeo-Christian West, "The Song of Songs").

If there is a theme that runs through the biographies—whether factual or legendary—of those women whose words have found a place in this book, it is that spiritual experience and "spirit" (in the sense of an animating courage) seem to go together. This should not surprise, given the etymological closeness of the words: both derive from the Latin word for breathing, and those who truly follow their own breath (the part of the self that is most tangibly at the same time ours and not-ours) will come to know both Being's nature and their own. And so, over and over in reading their stories, the reader will encounter women who broke with convention, who ignored cultural and religious taboo, who could not be held back from their chosen paths of life or spiritual practice.

A particularly fascinating example is an entire class of women who refused to be kept from the lives they most deeply desired: the Beguines, sometimes credited with inventing the first European women's movement. When, in the twelfth century, the Catholic Church refused to open new convents to house any additional women, in several northern European countries laywomen with a genuine vocation for religious life banded together to create their own forms of practice. They began by meeting several times daily for prayers, and by the time the movement reached its apex in the thirteenth and early fourteenth centuries some Beguinages had become virtual cities, housing up to fourteen thousand women and including hospitals, chapels, and even cathedrals within their walls.

The women who entered these communities took no formal vows, and had no official connection to the Church, but for the duration of their stay they observed the rules of chastity and poverty and the practice of charitable work. A widow might build herself a house within a Beguinage, enter it with only a few cooking utensils and a simple, nunlike habit, and remain there for the rest of her life, first caring for others, later being cared for. Or a young woman might enter a preexisting communal house and remain for a year or two within the community, later leaving to rejoin her family or perhaps to marry. Not surprisingly, a number of women mystics found their way into these places of refuge.

Many of the women in this book undertook more formal religious vows and training, as Catholic or Buddhist nuns, for example; yet they, too, quite often went through some period of difficult negotiation between outer and inner authority. Hildegard of Bingen, the famous eleventh-century German mystic and abbess, might easily have been excommunicated as a heretic because of her visions, had they not received the express endorsement of the pope. Teresa of Avila's writing was examined closely by the Inquisition, and she struggled at length with both Church and state authorities in the founding of each new convent of her order. Kassiane, a Greek Orthodox abbess of the ninth century, was flogged in her youth for assisting monks during a time of persecution. Antal, an eighth-century Tamil devotee of Krishna, unwittingly broke a strict taboo of his worship when she was a young child, yet, according to legend, was spared her father's anger by the direct intervention of Krishna on her behalf. Stories with a less happy outcome are those of Sor Juana, the seventeenth-century Mexican nun and woman of letters, whose outspoken defense of a full intellectual life for women eventually led to her being stripped of her books and her writing; and of Marguerite Porete, a French visionary, burned at the stake in the fourteenth century.

Other women included here lived independently as shamans or teachers. After liberation from slavery, the Persian Sufi Rabi'a eventually found her way to a one-room house on the outskirts of Basra, offering her guidance to the many adepts and ordinary people who sought out her wisdom.

Owl Woman, of the American Southwest, practiced as a healer within her home community after the spirit world began to give her sacred songs; Uvavnuk, an Iglulik Eskimo, became a shaman for her tribe after literally being struck by lightning; and several Chinese Taoists whose words are found here also taught independently, supporting themselves in the world however they could. One could even include among this company Emily Dickinson, dwelling in chosen isolation in her father's house in Amherst, and devoting herself to the making of poems offered only to a few friends and relatives.

Finally, there are women in this book who led lives for the most part typical of other women of their time and culture. Anne Bradstreet, a New England Puritan, was a devoted wife and mother. The Russian writers Akhmatova and Tsvetaeva experienced all the turmoil of the 1917 revolution and its effects on themselves, their families, and their country: one of Tsvetaeva's children starved to death, and the image of Akhmatova standing amid a crowd of other wives and mothers outside the walls of Lubyanka prison, holding a food bundle for her son, is known throughout the world. "Can you write about this?" she was asked, and she answered simply, "I can." Izumi Shikibu, companion to an empress of the Japanese court at the turn of the last millennium, married twice, had numerous love affairs, and was a mother who lived to see in her own daughter's death in childbirth a difficult confirmation of the Buddhist teaching of transience.

The social roles of men and women differ in every culture we know, and these distinctive cultural histories are undoubtedly reflected in the contents of this book; readers interested in this issue may compare for themselves the women's words and ways of speaking collected here with those in similar works by men. But the primary aim of this collection is not an exploration into questions of gender—it is rather to let these women speak for themselves of the experiences and issues of their spiritual lives, and to compensate for the all too frequent omission of women's voices from the wide chorus of the world's sacred singing. The wisdom and beauty they contain will, I hope, be as meaningful to male readers as to female.

I like to imagine the kind of conversation that might take place among the women included in this book, could they meet. Despite the varying expressions and frames of their understanding—the full moon of enlightenment discovered within a person's own house or heart, or the divine presence experienced as mystical Husband and Lover, whether Krishna or Christ, or the representation of ecstatic realization as a universe whose ordinary laws of physics and perception are turned utterly inside out—I believe that each one might recognize in the others something she knew to be close to her own life. In the poems they have left behind, as Hildegard of Bingen wrote, "the world-tree is blossoming"—a fragrance everywhere unique and the same.

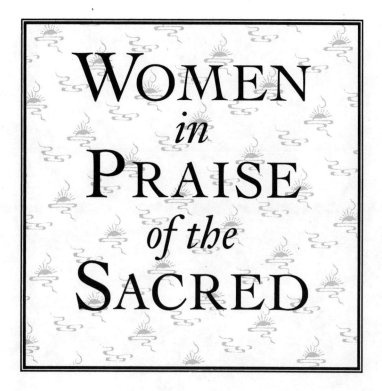

WOMEN
in
PRAISE
of the
SACRED

Enheduanna

(ca. 2300 B.C.E.)

Enheduanna is the earliest identified author of either sex in world literature. Daughter of the Sumerian king Sargon (whose domain lay in what is now southern Iraq), she was a high priestess in the service of the moon-god and moon-goddess, Nanna and Inanna. A number of Enheduanna's hymns have survived on cuneiform-inscribed tablets, and her portrait was found on a limestone disc during excavations of the city of Ur.

The Nin-me-sar-ra, excerpted here, tells the story of a time of political unrest when Enheduanna was cast into exile. Although the priestess appealed first to the god Nanna for help, it was his daughter Inanna who ultimately restored her to her rightful position; while other material about Inanna (see pages 8–10) depicts a goddess of eros and fertility, this hymn praises the moon-goddess primarily for the fierceness that accompanies her power and beauty. The hymn is believed to describe a shift in Inanna's rank to a higher position within the Sumerian pantheon, as well as a shift in power relations between human rulers. It is also the sole representation in this book of the fierce female energy found in spiritual traditions throughout the world. In figures ranging from the Hindu destroyer-goddess Kali to the Hawaiian Pele, we see how this destructive goddess-energy creates a necessary balance—for if the entrance to life is through the maternal feminine, the gates of death (dependent on prior earthly existence) must also be an aspect of engendering female power. There can be no genuine beauty or harmony that does not acknowledge the opposite powers of anger, fierceness, and destruction, the plot of this hymn tells us: a true spirituality includes all of life's aspects, not only those we find pleasing or simple.

from The Hymn to Inanna

Lady of all powers,
In whom light appears,
Radiant one
Beloved of Heaven and Earth,
Tiara-crowned
Priestess of the Highest God,
My Lady, you are the guardian
Of all greatness.
Your hand holds the seven powers:
You lift the powers of being,
You have hung them over your fingers,
You have gathered the many powers,
You have clasped them now
Like necklaces onto your breast.

————

Like a dragon,
You poisoned the land—
When you roared at the earth
In your thunder,
Nothing green could live.
A flood fell from the mountain:
You, Inanna,
Foremost in Heaven and Earth.
Lady riding a beast,
You rained fire on the heads of men.
Taking your power from the Highest,
Following the commands of the Highest,
Lady of all the great rites,
Who can understand all that is yours?

————

In the forefront
Of the battle,
All is struck down by you—
O winged Lady,
Like a bird
You scavenge the land.
Like a charging storm
You charge,
Like a roaring storm
You roar,
You thunder in thunder,
Snort in rampaging winds.
Your feet are continually restless.
Carrying your harp of sighs,
You breathe out the music of mourning.

———————

It was in your service
That I first entered
The holy temple,
I, Enheduanna,
The highest priestess.
I carried the ritual basket,
I chanted your praise.
Now I have been cast out
To the place of lepers.
Day comes,
And the brightness
Is hidden around me.
Shadows cover the light,
Drape it in sandstorms.
My beautiful mouth knows only confusion.
Even my sex is dust.

———————

What once was chanted of Nanna,
Let it now be yours—
That you are as lofty as Heaven,
Let it be known!
That you are as wide as the Earth,
Let it be known!
That you devastate the rebellious,
Let it be known!
That you roar at the land,
Let it be known!
That you rain your blows on their heads,
Let it be known!
That you feast on corpses like a dog,
Let it be known!
That your glance is lifting toward them,
Let it be known!
That your glance is like striking lightning,
Let it be known!
That you are victorious,
Let it be known!
That this is not said of Nanna,
It is said of you—
This is your greatness.
You alone are the High One.

———

O my Lady,
Beloved of Heaven,
I have told your fury truly.
Now that her priestess
Has returned to her place,
Inanna's heart is restored.
The day is auspicious,
The priestess is clothed
In beautiful robes,
In womanly beauty,

As if in the light of the rising moon.
The gods have appeared
In their rightful places,
The doorsill of Heaven cries "Hail!"
Praise to the destroyer endowed with power,
To my Lady enfolded in beauty.
Praise to Inanna.

Shu-Sin's Ritual Bride,
a Priestess of Inanna

(ca. 2000 B.C.E.)

*One of the central myths of ancient Sumer was the story of Inanna and Dumuzi
(the biblical Ishtar and Tammuz). Dumuzi, a human shepherd, woos and wins
the love of the moon/fertility goddess Inanna, and their blissful sexual union fruc-
tifies the earth. Later, however, he is offered as a sacrifice by Inanna in order to win
back her own freedom after she has recklessly gone down to the Underworld hoping
to add it to her domain of power; only Dumuzi's sister's willingness to take his place
results in the final compromise wherein each of the siblings spends half the year in
life and half in death. As in the later Greek myth of the earth-goddess Demeter
mourning her daughter Persephone, the season of winter has its origins then in
Inanna's belated grief each year at her husband's fate.*

*In order to ensure Sumer's fertility and prosperity, the marriage of Inanna
and Dumuzi was reenacted each New Year in a sacred marriage rite involving the
reigning king and a priestess-devotee of Inanna. The poem that appears here was
written by one such priestess, possibly Kubatum, whose inscribed necklace—a gift
from Shu-Sin—has been found in a temple excavation; or possibly Kubatum's
serving girl Il-ummiya. In this section of the ceremony, Inanna has been won over
by the king's eager entreaties and invites him (with an erotic enthusiasm that per-
meates the Inanna-Dumuzi literature) to consummate their union.*

*According to some scholars, it is in the tradition of Sumerian ritual courtship
and marriage songs that the roots of the biblical "Song of Songs" (see pages 22–27)
can most likely be found. One detail common to both can be seen in the excerpts
here; in both poems, obtaining the blessing of parental figures is included as part of
the consummation of divine love—a symbol, perhaps, for the necessity of including
and honoring the gifts of earthly, secular life in spiritual experience.*

Bridegroom, beloved of my heart,
Your pleasure is my pleasure, honey sweet;
Lion, beloved of my heart,
Your pleasure is my pleasure, honey sweet.

You have won my soul, I stand now trembling before you,
Bridegroom, carry me now to the bed.
You have won my soul, I stand now trembling before you,
Lion, carry me now to the bed.

Bridegroom, let me give you my caresses,
My sweet one, wash me with honey—
In the bed that is filled with honey,
Let us enjoy our love.
Lion, let me give you my caresses,
My sweet one, wash me with honey.

Bridegroom, now we have taken our pleasure,
Tell my mother, she will give you sweets,
Tell my father, he will give you gifts.

Your spirit—do I not know how to please it?
Bridegroom, sleep in our house till dawn.
Your heart—do I not know how to warm it?
Lion, sleep in our house till dawn.

Because you love me,
Lion, give me your caresses—
My husband and guardian, my spirit magician,
My Shu-Sin who gladdens the Wind-God's heart—
Give me your caresses because you love me.

The place sweet as honey, put in your sweetness—
Like flour into the measure, squeeze in your sweetness—
Like pounding dry flour into the cup to be measured,
Pound in, pound in your sweetness—

These words I sing for Inanna.

Makeda, Queen of Sheba

(ca. 1000 B.C.E.)

The Kebra Nagast, *an ancient Abyssinian chronicle of the Ethiopian royal lineage, contains an account of the meeting between the Queen of Sheba and King Solomon of ancient Israel that is also described in the Bible. According to both versions of the story, when Queen Makeda (renowned for her beauty, purity, and love of wisdom) learned of the wise king to the north of her country, she determined to find out if in truth he was as great in wisdom as reputed. She traveled to his court carrying many chests of gold and jewels and—entirely won over after testing him thoroughly—soon offered him the treasure she had brought and took up belief in the One God. The Bible then tells us that Solomon in turned granted her "all that she desired," and she returned to her own land.*

In the far more detailed Abyssinian account, we are told that Queen Makeda remained at Solomon's court for more than six months. When she decided to return to her country, Solomon—"a great lover of women" and husband to four hundred queens and six hundred concubines—could not bear to let the beautiful virgin queen depart untouched, and so he decided to seduce her. He ordered an ornate feast, and promised Makeda that in attending it she would learn more about the wisdom involved in the proper administration of the kingdom. In each of the courses, however, there was a great deal of salt or vinegar or hot spices.

At the end of the evening, Solomon invited the Queen to rest in his bedchamber. She accepted only after extracting from him a promise that he would not take her by force while she slept. He gave his word, but asked her in turn to promise that neither would she take anything from his house without permission.

After a few hours of sleep the Queen awakened, raging with thirst, and slipped from the bed to drink from a pitcher of water. But before she could take the first sip, King Solomon, who had only been pretending to sleep, stopped her and asked if she was not breaking her vow—what, he asked this Queen of a desert kingdom, could be more precious than water? She acknowledged that it was so, but begged to drink—releasing him from his promise. After she had had her fill, she returned to the King's bed, and went back to her own country pregnant.

Despite the fact that Queen Makeda appears to have been tricked, the Kebra Nagast account describes a meeting of equals, or at least near-equals. The Queen comes to Solomon's court as his peer in royal standing, from a country which she asserts is as wealthy as his own. Makeda's greatest love is wisdom, and her seduction, it is clear, is in wisdom's service and toward wisdom's ends. She does not complain of the outcome but delights in it, and her entire kingdom benefits from her decision to "know" Solomon—whose role in this story is the transmission of the sacred—in body as well as mind. Her story tells us that while purity is to be valued, there is a time when full wisdom requires a decision outside of conventional morality.

That Makeda was not Solomon's victim is made even clearer by the next part of the chronicle. The son of their union, Menyelek, traveled as a young man to Israel to meet his father. Solomon and his court acknowledged him with joy, and when Menyelek returned to Ethiopia to establish it as a kingdom of Solomon's line, it was in the company of many of the courtiers' eldest sons. At that point, however, Solomon's earlier deception of Queen Makeda found its mirror in his son's behavior. By means of a subterfuge, the departing entourage took with them the Tabernacle, the physical embodiment of God's covenant with Israel, and from that time forward, the Tabernacle—and God's true Kingdom—resided in Ethiopia. Again we see that wisdom lives not only by "light," but also by the shadowy ways and skillful means of the Trickster.

We also see in this story an idea about wisdom which is pervasive, at least in the traditions of the West: that wisdom is not given but taken, that it is obtainable only by the breaking of a taboo, and that the price of knowledge is the end of virginity and innocence. As with Eve and the apple of knowledge, Prometheus and his gift to mankind of fire, and Pandora and her box, we see in Queen Makeda's story that the way to a full human knowing lies through transgression and the body, through bliss and suffering, through birth and death—a price that is paid again and again.

The first of the two selections here is taken from words spoken by Queen Makeda before her journey to Jerusalem; the second is from the welcome she gave the sons of Solomon's courtiers when they arrived at her palace with the returning Menyelek.

Wisdom is
sweeter than honey,
brings more joy
than wine,
illumines
more than the sun,
is more precious
than jewels.
She causes
the ears to hear
and the heart to comprehend.

I love her
like a mother,
and she embraces me
as her own child.
I will follow
her footprints
and she will not cast me away.

I fell
because of wisdom,
but was not destroyed:
through her I dived
into the great sea,
and in those depths
I seized
a wealth-bestowing pearl.

I descended
like the great iron anchor
men use to steady their ships
in the night on rough seas,
and holding up the bright lamp
that I there received,
I climbed the rope
to the boat of understanding.

While in the dark sea,
I slept,
and not overwhelmed there,
dreamt: a star
blazed in my womb.

I marveled
at that light,
and grasped it,
and brought it up to the sun.
I laid hold upon it,
and will not let it go.

Sappho

(7th c. B.C.E.)

Born on the Greek island of Lesbos, Sappho is the earliest woman poet in the central lineage of Western literature. With the exception of fragments which survived because they were quoted by other writers, her work was lost in the burning of the great library at Alexandria; yet her words have nonetheless remained continuously alive from her own day to ours. We know little of her personal life other than that she married and had one daughter, Kleis. Renowned leader of a group of women poet-students, Sappho celebrated the love of both men and women in her poems.

Underlying Sappho's first poem is a belief that also appears in the Sumerian sacred marriage poem on pages 9–10: that the divine shares our enjoyment of sensual pleasure and beauty and manifests itself through and in it. The idea that sacredness is immanent in the life of this earth alternates throughout both Eastern and Western spiritual traditions with belief in a transcendence separate from and outside of daily existence—a concept that often leads to a spiritual life of asceticism and world-denial. Yet a truly mature spirituality finally resolves this split. One hint of how this is done can be found in the fourteenth-century words of St. Catherine of Siena: "All the way to heaven is heaven." Another is contained in the statement of Lingzhao, an eighth-century Chinese woman and Zen master known to us primarily as Layman Pang's daughter: "The great Masters' entire teaching can be found on the tips of the ten-thousand grasses."

Leave Crete,
Aphrodite,
and come to this
sacred place
encircled by apple trees,
fragrant with offered smoke.

Here, cold springs
sing softly
amid the branches;
the ground is shady with roses;
from trembling young leaves,
a deep drowsiness pours.

In the meadow,
horses are cropping
the wildflowers of spring,
scented fennel
blows on the breeze.

In this place,
Lady of Cyprus, pour
the nectar that honors you
into our cups,
gold, and raised up for drinking.

Evening Star who gathers everything
Shining dawn scattered—
You bring the sheep and the goats,
You bring the child back to its mother.

(tr. by Diane Rayor)

Sumangalamata

(6th c. B.C.E.)

"Sumangala's Mother," the wife of a maker of hats and shade-umbrellas, was a member of the earliest community of women followers of the Buddha. Many of these Pali-speaking women left accounts of their practice in poems, which were then collected in a volume known as the Therigatha. *Sumangalamata's is notable for its beginning: a joyous shout at her newfound freedom from the obligations of ordinary life. It is not so much that such tasks and relationships were necessarily problems in themselves, but the attachment and distraction that they represented were; and, as much as anything, Sumangalamata's delight came from having the time and opportunity to devote herself wholly to meditation. Permission for women to join the male monks in their life of forest retreats was first won, legend has it, by the Buddha's aunt, who had raised him from infancy after the death of his mother.*

At last free,
at last I am a woman free!
No more tied to the kitchen,
stained amid the stained pots,
no more bound to the husband
who thought me less
than the shade he wove with his hands.
No more anger, no more hunger,
I sit now in the shade of my own tree.
Meditating thus, I am happy, I am serene.

Patacara

(6th c. B.C.E.)

The daughter of a banker, Patacara rejected her parents' choice of a husband and ran away with her lover, a family servant. When her first child was almost due, she tried to persuade her husband to accompany her to her parents' house but he, understandably, refused. She attempted the journey alone, but midway—just as her husband caught up with her—she gave birth, and the three returned to their own home.

When her second pregnancy was coming to term, the argument was repeated, and again Patacara slipped off by herself. This time, however, just after her husband found her in the forest during a raging storm, he was fatally bitten by a poisonous snake while gathering brush to make a shelter. She delivered her baby alone, and set off once again the next day, but during her attempt to cross a rain-swollen river with the two infants, both died.

Half-crazed with grief, Patacara made her way to her parents' village, only to be told that the family house had collapsed in the storm the night before, killing everyone inside. Now entirely mad and driven off by the villagers, she wandered helplessly, her clothing torn, her hair uncombed, until she happened to enter the grove where the Buddha was teaching. Seeing her, he said simply, "Sister, recover your presence of mind," and she did. Afterward, he explained the eightfold path of Buddhist practice, and Patacara asked to be ordained. Her poem—which, like Sumangalamata's, comes from the Therigatha—*tells the story of her subsequent practice of mindfulness meditation and ultimate experience of awakening.*

Patacara's poem shows us a theme common in stories of Buddhist enlightenment: that awakening often comes to the mind at a moment when it relinquishes both effort and daytime, purposive consciousness. Jusammi Chikako's poem on page 113 is another depiction of this idea, and the Taoist teacher Sun Bu-er's poem on page 73 speaks as well of the relationship between long effort and an experience of opening that, when it finally occurs, seems to come "of its own accord."

When they plow their fields
and sow seeds in the earth,
when they care for their wives and children,
young brahmans find riches.

But I've done everything right
and followed the rule of my teacher.
I'm not lazy or proud.
Why haven't I found peace?

Bathing my feet
I watched the bathwater
spill down the slope.
I concentrated my mind
the way you train a good horse.

Then I took a lamp
and went into my cell,
checked the bed,
and sat down on it.
I took a needle
and pushed the wick down.

When the lamp went out
my mind was freed.

(tr. by Susan Murcott)

Zi Ye

(6th–3rd c. B.C.E.)

*A collection of popular Chinese folk songs, the Zi Ye (formerly spelled Tzu Yeh)
poems were traditionally ascribed to a single woman poet of that name. The "yes"
of this poem, arising out of no nameable place or being, has a mysteriously moving
power.*

All night I could not sleep
because of the moonlight on my bed.
I kept on hearing a voice calling:
Out of Nowhere, Nothing answered "yes."

(tr. by Arthur Waley)

Song of Songs: The Shulammite

(ca. 3rd c. B.C.E.)

While scholars now debate the origin of these biblical songs, they were collected under the guise of being an exchange between King Solomon and a woman known as the Shulammite, and have been read for two millennia as spiritual allegory. One common interpretation has been that the songs are an illustration of the love of God and Israel; another is that they describe the mystical union that is possible between the individual soul and God; and we have already seen a possible source for the "Songs" in the Sumerian ritual wedding poem on pages 9–10.

The line between love poetry and sacred poetry is fluid not only in the Western tradition—which undoubtedly shows the broad influence of this particular body of work—but also in Eastern cultures. In the Tamil poet Antal's Tiruppavai *(see pages 39–41), for instance, we see another example of a poetic form that began in women's ritual songs of courtship and was then turned to religious uses; and in work by Mirabai and the other* bhakti *(devotional) poets of India, and by the Sufi poet Rabi'a, we also find the seeker and God portrayed as lover and Beloved in language that is openly erotic. Each of the two kinds of experience of union serves to illumine and enlarge our understanding of the other.*

The verses from the Song of Songs excerpted here are from those sections attributed to the Shulammite. They give us the voice of a woman refreshingly confident of her worth and powers and of the importance of her own active role in the fulfillment of her one great desire—to join with the Beloved. It is interesting to compare the woman of the Song of Songs with the Queen of Sheba: though their stories and situations are quite different, both were legendary consorts of Solomon, both were strongly independent-minded, and both were dark-skinned in color. Whether the similarities between the two represent an archetype or the trace of one or more historical women we cannot know.

from The Song of Songs

Song 1:5–6

I am dark, daughters of Jerusalem,
And I am beautiful!
Dark as the tents of Kedar, lavish
As Solomon's tapestries.

Do not see me only as dark. The sun
Has stared at me.

My brothers were angry with me.
They made me guard the vineyards.
I have not guarded my own.

(tr. by Ariel and Chana Bloch)

Song 3:1–5

At night on my bed I longed for
My only love.
I sought him, but did not find him.

I must rise and go about the city,
The narrow streets and squares, till I find
My only love.
I sought him everywhere
And could not find him.

Then the watchmen found me
As they went about the city.
"Have you seen him? Have you seen
The one I love?"

I had just passed them when I found
My only love.
I held him, I would not let him go
Until I brought him to my mother's house,
Into my mother's room.

Daughters of Jerusalem, swear to me
By the gazelles, by the deer in the field,
That you will never awaken love
Until it is ripe.

(tr. by Ariel and Chana Bloch)

Song 5:2–6

I was asleep but my heart stayed awake.
Listen!
My lover knocking:

"Open, my sister, my friend,
My dove, my perfect one!
My hair is wet, drenched
with the dew of night."

"But I have taken off my clothes,
How can I dress again?
I have bathed my feet,
Must I dirty them?"

My love reached in for the latch
And my heart
Beat wild.

I rose to open to my love,
My fingers wet with myrrh,
Sweet flowing myrrh
On the doorbolt.

I opened to my love
But he had slipped away.
How I wanted him when he spoke!

I sought him everywhere
But could not find him.
I called to him
But he did not answer.

Then the watchmen found me
As they went about the city.
They beat me, they bruised me
They tore the shawl from my shoulders,
Those watchmen of the walls.

Swear to me, daughters of Jerusalem!
If you find him now,
You must tell him
I am in a fever of love.

(tr. by Ariel and Chana Bloch)

Song 7:12–14

Come, my beloved,
Let us go out into the fields
And sleep all night among the flowering henna.

Let us go early to the vineyards
To see if the vine has budded,
If the blossoms have opened
And the pomegranate is in flower.

There I will give you my love.

The air is filled with the scent of mandrakes
And at our doors
Rich gifts of every kind,
New and old, my love,
I have hidden away for you.

(tr. by Ariel and Chana Bloch)

Pan Zhao

(48–117?)

The only woman to hold the post of official historian to the Imperial Court of the Han Dynasty, Pan Zhao (formerly spelled Pan Chao) was widowed at an early age. She is the most famous woman scholar of Chinese history; besides history and poetry she wrote as well a popular collection of Confucian Precepts for Women.

This poem (the only example of her verse that I have been able to find in English) seems to lend itself to both exoteric and esoteric interpretations. Whatever its hidden meanings, it appears also to praise the merits of a "woman's way" of wisdom—which, it implies, those of less-subtle insight may fail to recognize.

Needle and Thread

Tempered, annealed, the hard essence of autumn metals
finely forged, subtle, yet perdurable and straight,

By nature penetrating deep yet advancing by inches
to span all things yet stitch them up together,

Only needle-and-thread's delicate footsteps
are truly broad-ranging yet without beginning!

"Withdrawing elegantly" to mend a loose thread,
and restore to white silk a lamb's-down purity . . .

How can those who count pennies calculate their worth?
They may carve monuments yet lack all understanding.

(tr. by Richard Mather and Rob Swigart)

Gnostic Gospel: Nag Hammadi Library

(2nd–4th c.)

Buried in a jar at the foot of a cliff (probably to preserve them from destruction by more orthodox Christian believers), the Gnostic works contained in what is now called the Nag Hammadi Library were found in December 1945 by two illiterate Muslim brothers gathering nitrate to fertilize their fields. The text of "The Thunder: Perfect Mind," given here in excerpted form, is unlike any other material in the collection, and appears to derive from the female-centered Isis worship preceding Christianity. Although no author for this piece is known, other Gnostic texts are attributed to women, and women are known to have held positions of leadership in Gnostic communities.

In its presentation of truth through paradox, "The Thunder: Perfect Mind" is strongly reminiscent of numerous works in the Western tradition (such as chapter eight of the Book of Proverbs) in which a female Wisdom figure speaks; this kind of utterance appears as well in the "crazy wisdom" tradition found in Tibetan Buddhism (see Lakshminkara, pages 48–50), Chinese Chan and Taoism, Japanese Zen, and elsewhere. The attempt to express mystical realization can take many forms, but it seems that one of the ways the inexpressible is pointed toward worldwide is through an exclamation and litany of the impossible such as is seen here.

Along with "The Song of Songs," the two spirituals found on pages 185 and 187, and several pieces from indigenous traditions, this selection represents (in this book) the many anonymous works in whose creation women are likely to have participated.

from The Thunder: Perfect Mind

Sent from the Power,
I have come
to those who reflect upon me,
and I have been found
among those who seek me.
Look upon me,
you who meditate,
and hearers, hear.
Whoever is waiting for me,
take me into yourselves.
Do not drive me
out of your eyes,
or out of your voice,
or out of your ears.
Observe. Do not forget who I am.

For I am the first, and the last.
I am the honored one, and the scorned.
I am the whore and the holy one.
I am the wife and the virgin.
I am the mother, the daughter,
and every part of both.
I am the barren one who has borne many sons.
I am she whose wedding is great
and I have not accepted a husband.
I am the midwife and the childless one,
the easing of my own labor.
I am the bride and the bridegroom
and my husband is my father.
I am the mother of my father,
the sister of my husband;
my husband is my child.

My offspring are my own birth,
the source of my power,
what happens to me is their wish.

I am the incomprehensible silence
and the memory that will not be forgotten.
I am the voice whose sound is everywhere
and the speech that appears in many forms.
I am the utterance of my own name.

Why, you who hate me, do you love me,
and hate those who love me?
You who tell the truth about me, lie,
and you who have lied, now tell the truth.
You who know me, be ignorant,
and you who have not known me, know.

For I am knowledge and ignorance.
I am modesty and boldness.
I am shameless, I am ashamed.
I am strength and I am fear.
I am war and I am peace.

Give heed to me,
the one who has been everywhere hated
and the one who is everywhere loved.
I am the one they call Life,
the one you call Death.
I am the one they call Law,
the one you call Lawless.
I am the one you have scattered,
and you have gathered me together.
I am godless, and I am the one
whose God is great.
I am the one whom you have reflected upon

and the one you have scorned.
I am unlearned,
and from me all people learn.
I am the one from whom you have hidden
and the one to whom you reveal yourself.
Yet wherever you hide, I appear,
And wherever you reveal yourself,
there I will vanish.

Those who are close to me
have failed to know me,
and those who are far from me know me.
On the day when I am close to you,
that day you are far from me;
on the day when I am far from you,
that day I am close.

I am the joining and the dissolving.
I am what lasts, and what goes.
I am the one going down,
and the one toward whom they ascend.
I am the condemnation and the acquittal.
For myself, I am sinless,
and the roots of sin grow in my being.
I am the desire of the outer,
and control of the inner.
I am the hearing in everyone's ears,
I am the speech which cannot be heard.
I am the mute who is speechless,
great are the multitudes of my words.

Hear me in softness,
and learn me in roughness.
I am she who cries out,

and I am cast forth upon the face of the earth.
I prepare the bread and my mind within.
I am called truth.

You praise me and you whisper against me.
You who have been defeated,
judge before you are judged:
the judge and all judging exist inside you.
For what is inside you is what is outside you,
and the one who formed you on the outside
is the one who shaped you within.

And what you see outside you, you see within.
It is visible and it is your garment.

Give heed then, you hearers,
and you also, angels and those who have been sent,
and you spirits risen now from the dead.
I am the one who alone exists,
there is no one to judge me.
For though there is much sweetness
in passionate life, in transient pleasure,
finally soberness comes
and people flee to their place of rest.
There they will find me,
and live, and not die again.

A Roman Spell

(2nd–4th c.?)

One of the religious traditions in which women have participated since the earliest times is the realm of magic, spellbinding, and sorcery. The following words are taken from an inscription described by their translator as "a tablet inscribed by a young woman, compelling a divine spirit to bring her the man she desires to marry, using language reminiscent of the Septuagint." (Interestingly, a similar inscription exists in which it is the love of another woman that is requested.) The excerpted lines are those in which the spirit is described and called forth.

I bind you by oath, great, eternal, ever-eternal, all-powerful god who is superior to the gods above. I bind you by oath, creator of heaven and sea. I bind you by oath, the one who has passed through the pious. I bind you by oath, the one who has separated the sea with the staff . . . I bind you by oath, the one who made the ass stop giving birth. I bind you by oath, the one who separated light from darkness. I bind you by oath, the one who shattered the rocks. I bind you by oath, the one who broke the mountains asunder. I bind you by oath, the one who formed the earth upon her foundations. I bind you by oath in the holy name which is not to be uttered . . . I bind you by oath, the one who made the luminaries and stars in heaven through the voice of command so as to bring light to all men. I bind you by oath, the one who shook the entire world, who both over-turned and spewed out the mountains, the one who made all the earth tremble and renewed all the inhabitants. I bind you by oath, the one who made the signs in heaven, on earth and in the sea . . . I bind you by oath, the eternal god, the great god, the all-powerful, whom all the mountains and valleys in all the world feared, you through whom the lion releases his prey, the mountains, the earth and the sea tremble . . .

Now, Now, Quickly, Quickly.

(tr. by Ross S. Kraemer)

Sabina Lampadius

(fl. ca. 377)

A priestess in the mystery religion of Cybele and Attis in fourth-century Rome, Sabina was the daughter of C. Caeionius Rufius Volusianus Lampadius, a man known for his fierce advocacy of the pagan religion. She wrote this poem in Greek as part of the inscription placed on an altar she erected in the Vatican in the year 377.

    Rhea (an alternative name for Cybele) is the all-powerful Goddess of Earth. Known also as the Great Mother and Mother of All Gods, she is often depicted sitting on a throne flanked by two protector lions and holding a sheaf of wheat or a fruiting branch as the symbol of her fertility. Her lover Attis, also mentioned in the poem, was a young human shepherd from Phrygia. In the Roman myth we find duplicated the roles played earlier by Inanna and Dumuzi (see pages 9–10), and in its images the goddess of fertility appears once again in association with the lion. Wherever there is abundance, it seems, it will be accompanied by the forces of ecstatic devouring: the lion is the visible remnant of the goddess's fierce aspect portrayed in Enheduanna's "Hymn to Inanna" on pages 4–7. (It is interesting to notice how strongly this dual motif has persisted over time: it is preserved even in the lion-claw feet of certain eighteenth- and nineteenth-century dining-room tables.) And the figure of the human shepherd who in some way enters into the realm of the divine is of course echoed as well in Christ, often presented as the shepherd of his flock.

As a symbol
of sacred mysteries,
I, Sabina,
daughter of Lampadius
and so of an honorable person,
here erected
to Attis and Rhea
an altar forever.
Deo's orgies
and the terrifying
Hekate nights
I experienced.

*(tr. from the Dutch of Maarten J.
Vermaseren by A. M. H. Lemmers)*

Antal

(8th c.)

Antal, also known as Andal, is the only woman among the twelve Alvars (Tamil saints; literally, "those who dive deep") of South Indian Vishnu worship. According to legend, she was found lying beneath a sacred basil bush in his garden by Vishnucitta, also an Alvar, who raised her as his own daughter. While too young to understand that the offering of "used" flowers to a god was strictly forbidden, Antal would take the garland her father had prepared for the evening ritual and place it around her own neck, imagining it to be a bridal adornment for her marriage to her Lord, then replace it on the household altar. When Vishnucitta discovered what had been happening, he made his evening puja *without flowers, apologizing for his daughter's acts of desecration. But the god appeared to him that night in a dream, saying that the garlands Antal had worn were especially dear to him, as they carried her fragrance, and that he wished the offering returned.*

Antal continued to be devoted only to Vishnu and refused to consider marriage to any human husband. When she was fifteen, her adopted father dreamt that Vishnu had accepted Antal in marriage. She traveled in full bridal regalia to the temple at Srirankam, walked into the arms of a statue of Vishnu reclining, and vanished.

Antal left two sets of poems, a group of hymns of devotional longing and the Tiruppavai, a poem in thirty stanzas whose annual recitation over the course of a month is still a part of Tamil Vishnu worship. It is based on a courtship ritual in which young girls would rise each dawn for the month of Markali (mid-December to mid-January) and bathe in cold rivers, ponds, or lakes, reciting poems in which they asked the water-gods for marriage to a man who was a fine lover and with whom they would bear many children. In Antal's poem, this ritual is transformed into a drought-ending rite of bathing (a word with sexual connotations in the poem) to be performed by the god Krishna and the Gopis, the cowherding girls of the village who had until then been kept separate from the handsome god by their concerned parents.

Over the course of the poem, the speaker travels from house to house, awaken-

ing each of the other girls in turn and encouraging her to join the group for the rite. *(Each household's occupant represents a different human trait—laziness, beauty, wealth, religious devotion, and so on—whose "door" must be opened for awakening to occur.) They then go to the house in which Krishna sleeps, where they awaken first his in-laws, then his wife (whom they soundly rebuke for behaving in a manner "unfitting her nature" by holding him back from them), and finally the god himself.*

The three sections of the Tiruppavai *given here show the Gopis first coming to the house of one of their group, then arriving at Krishna's father-in-law's house, then, in the penultimate stanza of the poem, speaking directly to the god.*

from The Tiruppavai

12.

O sister of wealth,
you whose lowing buffalo
yearn for their calves
so greatly the rich milk falls
from their udders untouched
to a milk-muddied floor,
we stand at your closed door
drenched in morning dew.
We sing the praises of our Beloved,
to tell here of his wrath
that destroyed the cruel Southern King.
How can you go on sleeping
when all of us are awake?
Wake up! Speak now and join us, hear our song!

16.

O you who guard over
and watch the mansion's gates,
who keep safe the carved arches,
the colorful flags, let us in!
Unlatch the jewel-studded door!
The sapphire-bodied lord of illusion
only yesterday offered his word:
he would give us the Inner Drum.
We girls have come here
only to sing him awake,
do not refuse our request.
O good sirs, the doors that are closed
and locked on tightly shut hinges
must open! Please let us in, hear our song!

29.

We rose before dawn
to praise you,
bringing our song to your Lotus Feet—
hear what we ask!
Please listen,
you who were born among us
into this cowherding clan—
What choice do you have
but to take us into your service,
your heartfelt servants, your kin?
We didn't come to receive the outer drum,
the drum of a day, O Govinda—
We are yours for life.
Make all our desires be for you,
it is you alone that we want. Hear our song!

Rabi'a

(717–801)

The fourth daughter of a poor family, the Persian Sufi Rabi'a was born in the city of Basra, in what is now Iraq. Orphaned early when her parents died of famine, and separated from her sisters, she was taken captive in the street and sold into a life of slavery. For years she fasted and prayed as she performed her duties, until finally, according to legend, her master awakened one night to see an unearthly lamp shining above her and lighting the entire house while she was at prayer; the next morning, he freed her. She went first to the desert to live in seclusion, and later built a small retreat house on the outskirts of Basra.

Although she received offers of marriage from both men of secular power and spiritual leaders, Rabi'a chose the life of a celibate ascetic. Her fame as a mystic and teacher spread widely, and many people came to her home to study with her, to ask her spiritual advice, and to record her words. One visitor described what he found this way: "In her entire house I saw only the pitcher with a chipped spout which she used for bathing as well as drinking water, the brick which she used as a pillow, and the reed mat on which she prayed. Other than this, there was nothing. Whatever people tried to give her, she rejected, saying only, 'I have no need of the world.'"

Rabi'a's poems and the stories we have of her life show us a woman whose spiritual authority derived from her utter confidence in surrendering her own will to that of the divine. One story tells of the time when her donkey died in the middle of the desert while Rabi'a was on pilgrimage to Mecca; she refused the help of her traveling companions and stayed alone by the animal's body, only asking her Lord whether or not he wished her to visit his House. The donkey then sprang back to his feet, and the two continued on their way. Even beyond surrender, though, the deepest note of Rabi'a's poems is one of intimacy and adoration: her trust in her Lord is unbounded because her love for Him is unbounded.

I am fully qualified to work as a doorkeeper, and for this reason:
What is inside me, I don't let out;
What is outside me, I don't let in.
If someone comes in, he goes right out again—
He has nothing to do with me at all.
I am a Doorkeeper of the Heart, not a lump of wet clay.

(tr. by Charles Upton)

O my Lord,

if I worship you
from fear of hell, burn me in hell.

If I worship you
from hope of Paradise, bar me from its gates.

But if I worship you
for yourself alone, grant me then the beauty of your Face.

O my Lord,
the stars glitter
and the eyes of men are closed.
Kings have locked their doors
and each lover is alone with his love.

Here, I am alone with You.

Yeshe Tsogyel

(757?–817?)

Yeshe Tsogyel is the foremost woman in the history of Tibetan Buddhism. Her poetry and history have come down to us in the form of a biographical terma (a sacred document hidden for later revelation). According to this account, Tsogyel was born a princess. She hoped to avoid marriage, fleeing all suitors, but was wed at the age of twelve to a king, who then relinquished her to the Buddhist teacher Padmasambhava in return for his teaching.

Protests on the part of government officials who practiced Bon (the indigenous religion of Tibet) soon forced the two to flee to the mountains, where they spent three years in meditation practice, leading to Tsogyel's full initiation. Her next task was to seek out her predestined spiritual consort, whom she found in Nepal and purchased out of slavery. The couple returned to Padmasambhava to practice further, and eventually teacher and disciples helped bring about the transition of the state religion to Buddhism. The rest of Tsogyel's life was spent in meditation and in instructing large numbers of men and women in the Way, thus helping to solidify the place of Buddhist teaching in Tibet.

Tsogyel's description of wisdom as residing not in any outer teaching but within the self's own experience is echoed in many other pieces in this book, not only in poems from Asian spiritual traditions, but also, strikingly, in the poetry of the Flemish Hadewijch II (see page 109).

Listen,
O brothers and sisters,
you who have mastered the teaching—
If you recognize me,
Queen of the Lake of Awareness,
who encompasses
both emptiness and form,
know that I live in the minds
of all beings who live.
Know that I live
in the body of mind
and the field of the senses,
that the twelve kinds of matter
are only my bones and my skin.
We are not two,
yet you look for me outside;
when you find me within yourself,
your own naked mind,
that Single Awareness
will fill all worlds.
Then the joy of the One
will hold you like a lake—
its fish with gold-seeing eyes
will grow many and fat.
Hold to that knowledge and pleasure,
and the Creative will be your wings.
You will leap through the green meadows
of earthly appearance,
enter the sky-fields, and vanish.

Lakshminkara

(8th c.)

Lakshminkara, a princess of northern India, was betrothed to the king of Sri Lanka when a wandering master introduced her to Tantric Buddhist practice. Upon learning that her prospective husband failed to share her desire for spiritual awakening, she broke off the engagement and took up instead the path of a solitary practitioner, living in caves and the forest. She became a highly influential teacher, and we have both practice manuals that she wrote for her disciples and several additional spiritual treatises in which she rejected formal religious ritual in favor of the non-dual, spontaneous expression of realized mind. Lakshminkara chose to retain one formal Tantric practice, however: the ritual in which a man pays homage to the woman who is his spiritual partner, making offerings to her and recognizing her as the living embodiment of the Buddha. It seems that she found this corrective to the prevailing inequality between the sexes indispensable to the full ripening of her students' understanding.

The doha, or ecstatic song, given here was uttered in front of two of Lakshminkara's disciples, the sisters Mekhala and Kanakhala, one of whom is addressed in the poem. It speaks from the state of what is called in the Tibetan tradition "crazy wisdom": in the mind free of dualistic thinking, where all things are one and interpenetrate each other fully, infinite realities are possible, and day-to-day perception is recognized as only one of many potential ways to understand the nature of phenomena. Perhaps the most appropriate response to such a realization is the one we see here: a shout of amazement and laughter.

Lay your head on a block of butter and chop—
Break the blade of the axe!
The woodcutter laughs!
A frog swallows an elephant!

It's amazing, Mekhala,
Do not doubt.
If it confounds you, o seeker,
Drop concepts now!

My teacher didn't tell me,
I didn't understand—
Flowers blossomed in the sky!

It's marvelous, Mekhala,
Have no doubt!
If you're incredulous, adept,
Drop your doubts!

A barren woman gives birth!
A chair dances!
Because cotton is expensive,
The naked weep!

. . . .

Amazing! An elephant sits on a throne
Held up by two bees!
Incredible! The sightless lead,
The mute speak!

. . . .

Amazing! A mouse chases a cat!
An elephant flees from a crazy donkey!

It's marvelous, Mekhala,
Do not doubt!
If you're stunned, adept,
Drop your doubts!

Amazing! A hungry monkey eats rocks!
Wonderful—the experience of the mind!
Who can express it?

(tr. by Miranda Shaw)

Three Tantric Buddhist Women's Songs

(8th–11th c.)

Upon coming into a state of awakened mind (often after years of disciplined practice), many women practitioners of Tantric Buddhism in India would spontaneously speak or sing of their experience, as Lakshminkara did in the preceding poem. These poems were recorded by others present at the time, and some have been preserved in volumes assembled by later Tibetan-speaking women—a rare example of women prior to our own time deliberately collecting the poetry and teaching of other women explicitly because they were women.

KYE HO! Wonderful!
Lotus pollen wakes up in the heart's center—
The bright flower is free from mud.
Where do the color and fragrance come from?
What reason now to accept them or turn away?

Kambala

Who speaks the sound of an echo?
Who paints the image in a mirror?
Where are the spectacles in a dream?
Nowhere at all—that's the nature of mind!

Tree-Leaf Woman

KYE HO! Wonderful!
You may say "existence," but you can't grasp it!
You may say "nonexistence," but many things appear!
It is beyond the sky of "existence" and "nonexistence"—
I know it but cannot point to it!

Dakini Lion-Face

(all tr. by Miranda Shaw)

Kassiane

(804?–?)

Kassiane is the best known Byzantine woman writer and the only one whose work is included in the Eastern Orthodox liturgy, where twenty-three of her hymns have found a place. Born in Constantinople to an aristocratic family, as a young woman she was publicly lashed for supporting exiled and imprisoned monks during a time when imperial edicts forbade Orthodox practices. (Other women who took part in the same movement were executed.) One early legend presents the youthful Kassiane also as an active defender of the inherent goodness of women in a culture that regularly condemned them as the source of original sin, and tells us that her forthright attitude when questioned on the subject caused the emperor's son to reject her as a potential bride.

In 843, Eastern Orthodoxy was reestablished as the state religion of Byzantium by the Empress Theodora. Kassiane became a nun at once and eventually founded a convent. Like the better-known Hildegard of Bingen two centuries later, she composed both the words and the music of hymns to be sung by the nuns under her direction. Also like Hildegard, she remained until her death an outspoken defender of her beliefs and ideals, writing, among a list of many similar statements, "I hate silence when it is time to speak."

Kassiane's hymn "Troparion" speaks in the voice of the "Sinful Woman," a figure derived from the Gospel of St. Luke: near the beginning of Jesus' public ministry, an anonymous harlot came uninvited to the house of Simon and asked to anoint Jesus' feet. When Simon questioned whether a true prophet would permit such a person to touch him, Jesus reprimanded him and absolved the woman of her sins, saying, "Your faith has saved you; go in peace." This hymn on the eternal possibility of repentance is sung during the week of Lent, on Holy Tuesday.

Troparion

                                        Lord,
This woman who encountered her shadow
    perceives the numinous in You,
    leads the women who come with grief
    and myrrh to Your grave.
Alas! What a desperate night I've traveled through:
    extravagant the desire, dark and moonless
    the needs of a passionate body.
Accept this spring of tears,
    You who empty the seawater from the clouds.
Bend to the pain in my heart, You
    whose incarnation bent the sky
    and left it empty.
I will wash your feet with kisses,
    dry them with my hair, feet that Eve once heard
    at dusk in Paradise then hid in fear.
You who are limitless mercy—who will trace the results
    of a lifetime I've done wrong, evaluate
    my weakness? I ask, remember me,
    if nothing else, as one who lived.

(tr. by Liana Sakelliou)

Yu Xuanji

(843?–868)

Born in the Chinese capital city of Chang An, Yu Xuanji (formerly spelled Yü Hsüan-chi) was a courtesan who became the second wife of Li Yi, a government official whose jealous first wife eventually drove her away. She then became a Taoist adept and teacher. Yu initially undertook strict ascetic practices, but later was forced to return to her earlier occupation of courtesan in order to support herself. Finally she was executed on a false charge of having murdered her maid.

Yu's description of a Taoist paradise is in poignant contrast with the details we know of most of her life. In her poem, the realm of ordinary human activities and that of the natural world share a deep accord, in which the poet's expression of her own inner nature can open as freely and easily as the wildflowers' blossoms. The image of the boat (which signifies Taoist-yogic practice) appears again in Li Qing-zhao's poem on page 65.

At Home in the Summer Mountains

I've come to the house of the Immortals:
In every corner, wildflowers bloom.
In the front garden, trees
Offer their branches for drying clothes;
Where I eat, a wine glass can float
In the springwater's chill.
From the portico, a hidden path
Leads to the bamboo's darkened groves.
Cool in a summer dress, I choose
From among heaped piles of books.
Reciting poems in the moonlight, riding a painted boat . . .
Every place the wind carries me is home.

Izumi Shikibu

(974?–1034?)

Considered the greatest woman poet of Japanese literature, Izumi Shikibu was part of the only Golden Age in world literature that was created by women writers. She served as a companion to an empress of the imperial court at Heian-kyo (present-day Kyoto), married young, and gave birth to a daughter, but soon created a great scandal when she abandoned her husband to begin a relationship with the empress's son. After his death, his brother, Prince Atsumichi, became the great love of her life. After Prince Atsumichi's death five years later, Shikibu took many lovers before marrying for a second time and moving from the capital to the provinces with her new husband.

Shikibu's poetry shows a commitment not only to a life of eros, but also to Buddhist teaching and practice: a good number of her poems were written during retreats at mountain temples, and many, whatever their ostensible subject, show both keen personal awareness of transience and study of the sutras. To read her poems (and those of the other Japanese women in this book as well), it is helpful to know that in Buddhist cultures the moon is often a symbol of awakened mind. In the first poem given here, we can then see, the subject is the unity of the small, transient flower of the daily world and the experience of enlightenment: the moon— and the mind of realization—are not distant and unreachable, the poem tells us, but exist fully in the things of this earth when they are understood in their true nature.

The third poem also deserves comment. The voices of the crickets outside the monastery are of course the voices of "the world," of the events and people of Shikibu's ordinary life, as well as actual crickets. But this does not mean the poet necessarily believed in any simple way that to be a good Buddhist requires ignoring their cries; one of the most important ideals in Japanese Buddhism is found in the female figure of Kannon, the Bodhisattva whose Sanskrit name, Avalokitesvara, means "The One Who Hears the Cries of the World." Izumi Shikibu offers us an example of a person whose Buddhism was realized fully in the realm of everyday life, in the midst of the heart's cries.

I cannot say
which is which:
the glowing
plum blossom *is*
the spring night's moon.

*(tr. by Jane Hirshfield
and Mariko Aratani)*

Watching the moon
at midnight,
solitary, mid-sky,
I knew myself completely,
no part left out.

*(tr. by Jane Hirshfield
and Mariko Aratani)*

In the autumn, on retreat at a mountain temple

Although I try
to hold the single thought
of Buddha's teaching in my heart,
I cannot help but hear
the many crickets' voices calling as well.

(tr. by Jane Hirshfield and Mariko Aratani)

Although the wind
blows terribly here,
the moonlight also leaks
between the roof planks
of this ruined house.

*(tr. by Jane Hirshfield
and Mariko Aratani)*

The way I must enter
leads through darkness to darkness—
O moon above the mountains' rim,
please shine a little further
on my path.

(tr. by Jane Hirshfield and Mariko Aratani)

Ly Ngoc Kieu

(1041–1113)

Also known as Dieu Nhan, Ly Ngoc Kieu was a Zen Buddhist nun in eleventh-century Vietnam. Eldest daughter of Prince Phung Can Vuong and goddaughter of a king, she was married to a district chief; after she became a widow, she took religious vows. The earliest known woman writer of Vietnam, she served as the director of a temple, Huong Hai, for many years.

Birth, old age,
Sickness, and death:
From the beginning,
This is the way
Things have always been.
Any thought
Of release from this life
Will wrap you only more tightly
In its snares.
The sleeping person
Looks for a Buddha,
The troubled person
Turns toward meditation.
But the one who knows
That there's nothing to seek
Knows too that there's nothing to say.
She keeps her mouth closed.

(tr. by Thich Nhat Hanh and Jane Hirshfield)

Li Qingzhao

(1084–1151?)

Considered China's greatest woman poet, Li Qingzhao (formerly spelled Li Ch'ing-chao) came from a family of high standing in both government and the arts. Her father and his circle of literary friends welcomed and encouraged her early interest in poetry (an unusual circumstance for a girl in China in that period), as did her husband, the scholar Zhao Mingcheng. Along with Zhao, she pursued her interests in painting, calligraphy, stone-rubbings of ancient inscriptions, and ancient inscribed bronzes—all intellectual activities usually restricted to men—and her poems demonstrate a similarly passionate inquiry into the realm of politics and the natural world.

The tumultuous political upheavals of Sung China eventually disrupted this happy life. Many of Li's later years were spent fleeing various warring factions, and eventually the large collection of artworks that she and her husband had assembled was entirely lost. After her husband's death, she is thought to have married a second time, this time a man who abused both Li and his government position. Her accusations against him sent him to prison, but resulted in her own incarceration as well: guilt by relationship has been, sadly, a long-standing tradition in China. She is believed to have spent her final years in the home of a younger brother, and died around the age of sixty-eight.

Biographies do not indicate where or how Li Qingzhao came by the training in Taoist Yoga that is clearly reflected in the imagery of this poem, which is quite unlike any of the rest of her work. Kenneth Rexroth has suggested that the "inner bird" (literally, "roc bird") symbolizes the autonomic nervous system, that the boat is a vehicle for the "Serpent Power" contained at the base of the spine, and that the Immortal Islands are a traditional image for the thousand-petaled lotus of realization.

Written to the Tune
"The Fisherman's Honor"

The sky becomes one with its clouds,
the waves with their mist.
In Heaven's starry river, a thousand sails dance.
As if dreaming, I return to the place
where the Highest lives,
and hear a voice from the heavens:
Where am I going?
I answer, "The road is long,"
and sigh; soon the sun will be setting.
Hard to find words in poems to carry amazement:
on its ninety-thousand-mile wind,
the huge inner bird is soaring.
O wind, do not stop—
My little boat of raspberry wood
has not yet reached the Immortal Islands.

Hildegard of Bingen

(1098–1179)

*One of the most famous of all Western women mystics, Saint Hildegard—the
tenth child of her parents—was "tithed" to God at the age of eight, when she was
sent to live in the Benedictine community of a local holy woman, Jutta. From ear-
liest childhood Hildegard experienced both clairvoyance and waking visions, and
at the age of five she accurately predicted the markings of an as yet unborn calf.
Hildegard soon learned to conceal her special gifts, and it was only when she had
reached the age of forty-two, five years after she had become abbess of the convent
that had evolved out of Jutta's community, that a voice commanded her to make
her experiences known. In her old age, she described her visual field as having con-
tained at all times a backdrop of radiance on which her visions were projected; she
called this phenomenon the "shadow of the living Light."*

Hildegard's first book, the Scivias, *was written over a period of ten years, dur-
ing which time the authenticity of her visions and teaching was affirmed by both
Bernard of Clairvaux and Pope Eugenius III. She soon became famous even be-
yond Germany, and her advice was sought by clerics, common people, and reigning
potentates throughout Europe. At the age of sixty, in an unprecedented activity for
a woman, she undertook the first of the four preaching tours which she made, de-
spite frequent illness, over the course of her long life.*

*Hildegard was an able leader of her community, attending carefully to the
needs of her nuns, and also participated actively in the political life of her time,
even chastising the Holy Roman Emperor Frederick I for endorsing a false pope.
The corpus of her works includes not only detailed accounts and paintings of her
visions but also two lengthy treatises on natural science, medicine, ethics, and cos-
mology. Feminine imagery of the divine is pervasive in both Hildegard's illumi-
nations and her words, and she describes Eve, Mary, and the Church-as-Mother
as essential figures in God's plan for the redemption of the world.*

The poems found here come from the Symphony of the Harmony of Celes-
tial Revelations. *They were written in Latin as part of the liturgy for the nuns,
and sung to music which was also of Hildegard's own composition. As the title of the*

collection implies, Hildegard attributed both music and words (each highly unusual) to a divine source; she described herself in a letter to her fellow mystic Elisabeth of Schönau as only "God's trumpet," the instrument through which his voice could be heard.

Antiphon for Divine Wisdom

Sophia!
you of the whirling wings,
circling encompassing
energy of God:

you quicken the world in your clasp.

One wing soars in heaven
one wing sweeps the earth
and the third flies all around us.

Praise to Sophia!
Let all the earth praise her!

(tr. by Barbara Newman)

Antiphon for the Holy Spirit

The Spirit of God
is a life that bestows life,
root of world-tree
and wind in its boughs.

Scrubbing out sin,
she rubs oil into wounds.

She is glistening life
alluring all praise,
all-awakening,
all-resurrecting.

(tr. by Barbara Newman)

Antiphon for the Angels

Spirited light! on the edge
of the Presence your yearning
burns in the secret darkness,
O angels, insatiably
into God's gaze.

Perversity
could not touch your beauty;
you are essential joy.
But your lost companion,
angel of the crooked
wings—he sought the summit,
shot down the depths of God
and plummeted past Adam—
that a mud-bound spirit might soar.

(tr. by Barbara Newman)

Song to the Creator

You, all-accomplishing
Word of the Father,
are the light of primordial
daybreak over the spheres.
You, the foreknowing
mind of divinity,
foresaw all your works
as you willed them,
your prescience hidden
in the heart of your power,
your power like a wheel around the world,
whose circling never began
and never slides to an end.

(tr. by Barbara Newman)

Alleluia-verse for
the Virgin

Alleluia! light
burst from your untouched
womb like a flower
on the farther side
of death. The world-tree
is blossoming. Two
realms become one.

(tr. by Barbara Newman)

Kojijū

(1121? – 1201?)

Kojijū was the daughter of the director of the Iwashimizu Hachiman Shrine in Kyoto. During her long life she served first in the retinue of an empress and later an emperor; in 1179, she became a Buddhist nun. She was also an active member of the poetic revival which took place at the end of the twelfth century. Her poem reflects the Buddhist teaching that enlightenment is innate: not something to be looked for outside ourselves, but always already present, waiting to be seen at any moment.

On the Spirit of the Heart as Moon-Disk

Merely to know
The Flawless Moon dwells pure
 In the human heart
Is to find the Darkness of the night
Vanished under clearing skies.

(*tr. by Edwin A. Cranston*)

Sun Bu-er

(1124–?)

The most famous woman teacher of Chinese Taoism, Sun Bu-er (formerly spelled Sun Pu-erh) was born in 1124. Married to another Taoist practitioner who is also said to have achieved complete realization, she bore and raised three children before turning to full-time practice of the Way at the age of fifty-one. She later taught other women initiates, and a number of the treatises she wrote for them have survived. In Taoist folklore, she is known as one of the Seven Immortals.

Like Patacara's poem on page 20, Sun Bu-er's first poem speaks of the relationship between effort and the realization already everywhere present. In the second poem, the "hidden cottage" is the dwelling-place of a Taoist hermit; for the symbolic meaning of apricot blossoms, see page 76.

Cut brambles long enough,
Sprout after sprout,
And the lotus will bloom
Of its own accord:
Already waiting in the clearing,
The single image of light.
The day you see this,
That day you will become it.

Late Indian summer's
Soft breezes fanning out,
The sun shines
On the hidden cottage
South of the river.
December, and the apricots'
First flowers open.
A person looks,
The blossoms look back:
Plain heart seeing into plain heart.

Zhou Xuanjing

(12th c.)

Another Chinese Taoist adept, Zhou Xuanjing's (formerly spelled Chou Hsüan-ching) curiosity about the Way was first awakened when she dreamt that she was immersed in a scarlet mist (considered an auspicious sign) just before the birth of her son Wang Chuyi, who would eventually become a teacher of the highest rank. When he began Taoist study at the age of twenty, Zhou became a disciple of the same teacher, and was later given the title "Free Human of Mystic Peace."

Meditating at midnight,
Meditating at noon,
A mind like autumn
Comes to the Way's deep heart.
Under motionless waves,
Fish and dragons freely leap.
In the sky without limits,
Only the moonlight stays.

Cui Shaoxuan

(dates unknown)

Beyond the fact that she was a teacher of Taoism, all we know of Cui Shaoxuan (formerly spelled Ts'ui Shao–hsüan) is that she was the youngest daughter of a provincial government official in Northern China. The apricot blossoms in this poem are a traditional symbol (along with plum blossoms, also among the first to bloom) for the opening of innate awakened mind after the stillness and cold of a state of deep concentration. A famous description of this process by the thirteenth-century Japanese Zen master Dōgen comes to mind: "It is out of bone-freezing winter that the plum blossoms bloom—spring rubs hard at the nostrils." Any gardener can attest to the accuracy of the metaphor: without the requisite number of hours of winter-chill, fruit trees will not bear.

Black hair and red cheeks: for how long?
One moment, and the silver threads run through.
Open the blinds: the first apricot blossoms have opened—
Hurry! The spring days are now!

Mahadeviyakka

(12th c.)

Mahadeviyakka was born in the Indian village of Udatadi, and wrote in the Kannada dialect. A disciple of Shiva and the path of Oneness from the age of ten, she was forcibly married to the local ruler—a Jain—but left him to take up again the life of an ecstatic devoted only to Shiva, whom she addresses in her poems as her White Jasmine Lord and only truly satisfactory lover. Like several other bhakti *(devotional) poets in this collection, she gave up conventional dress along with conventional life, and traveled the countryside alone. Stories say that when she died in her twenties she disappeared into a burst of light.*

Mahadeviyakka's abiding theme is the complete sufficiency of her experience of the oneness of self and the divine. The vulnerability she espouses in the third poem is reminiscent of Izumi Shikibu's poem on page 61; by exposing ourselves to a life without shelter and risking hunger, cold, and loneliness, the poem says, we also allow a sense of the sacred to enter our lives. And the last line of her poem on page 84— "What use for words at all?"—is echoed by other women throughout this book, including Ly Ngoc Kieu, Lakshminkara, and Mechtild of Magdeburg. Again and again, these poets, teachers, and singers come to the point where they confess the inability of any language to hold the uncontainable, inexpressible core.

(On Her Decision to
Stop Wearing Clothes)

Coins in the hand
Can be stolen,
But who can rob this body
Of its own treasure?

The last thread of clothing
Can be stripped away,
But who can peel off Emptiness,
That nakedness covering all?

Fools, while I dress
In the Jasmine Lord's morning light,
I cannot be shamed—
What would you have me hide under silk
And the glitter of jewels?

So long as this breath fills your nostrils,
Why seek out fragrant flowers?

Peaceful, compassionate, patient, already your own master,
Why do you need to cross your legs to Know?

Once the entire world is yourself,
What could a life of solitude add?

O white Jasmine Lord—

cross your legs: the traditional lotus posture of meditation

When I am hungry,
The villagers
Fill my begging bowl
With rice.

Thirsty, I turn toward
The cattle troughs, wells,
And streams.

For my sleep,
Abandoned temples
Are blanket enough.

And when I am lonely,
O white Jasmine Lord,
My soul deepens
with You.

A vein of sapphires
hides in the earth,
a sweetness in fruit;

and in plain-looking rock
lies a golden ore,
and in seeds,
the treasure of oil.

Like these,
the Infinite
rests concealed in the heart.

No one can see the ways
of our jasmine-white Lord.

It was like a stream
    running into the dry bed
    of a lake,

        like rain
    pouring on plants
    parched to sticks.

It was like this world's pleasure
    and the way to the other,
                    both
    walking toward me.

Seeing the feet of the master,
O lord white as jasmine,
    I was made
    worthwhile.

(tr. by A. K. Ramanujan)

When the body becomes Your mirror,
how can it serve?

When the the mind becomes Your mind,
what is left to remember?

Once my life is Your gesture,
how can I pray?

When all my awareness is Yours,
what can there be to know?

I became You, Lord, and forgot You.

I do not call it his sign,
I do not call it becoming one with his sign.
I do not call it union,
I do not call it harmony with union.
I do not say something has happened,
I do not say nothing has happened.
I will not name it You,
I will not name it I.
Now that the White Jasmine Lord is myself,
What use for words at all?

Mechtild of Magdeburg

(1207?–1282? or 1297?)

Daughter of a wealthy German family, Mechtild of Magdeburg's first intimation of her future came at the age of twelve, when she saw "all things in God, and God in all things." In 1235 she entered a local house of the Beguines, independent communities of laywomen devoted to leading a life of good works, poverty, chastity, and spiritual practice. (For a further description of the Beguines, see the Preface.) There, after she had recovered from a severe illness, a voice instructed her to undertake a written description of the revelations she received over the next fourteen years; she called the resulting work The Flowing Light of the Godhead.*

Though the Low German original has been lost, the book was preserved in an Allemanic translation, and an early version in Latin is said to have been an important influence upon Dante. In 1270, Mechtild took formal vows and entered the convent of Helfta, a center of both spirituality and learning known as the crown of all German convents. Her example and her writings (mostly completed before that time) were a major influence on the famous trio of visionary nuns residing there, the abbess Gertrude of Hackeborn, her sister Mechtild of Hackeborn, and the young postulant Gertrude the Great.

In Mechtild's poetry, as in that of many other women in this book from many different traditions, we find the encounter between self and Self depicted as a relationship of lovers. Her first poem brings vividly to mind the spinning-worship of Sufi dervishes—a surprising image from one who led the outwardly restrained life of a Beguine. But exuberance too is part of the mystic's path, and throughout Mechtild's work we find an energy and vigor that reflect the dynamic nature of her spiritual realization.

I cannot dance, O Lord,
Unless You lead me.
If You wish me to leap joyfully,
Let me see You dance and sing—

Then I will leap into Love—
And from Love into Knowledge,
And from Knowledge into the Harvest,
That sweetest Fruit beyond human sense.

There I will stay with You, whirling.

A fish cannot drown in water,
A bird does not fall in air.
In the fire of its making,
Gold doesn't vanish:
The fire brightens.
Each creature God made
Must live in its own true nature;
How could I resist my nature,
That lives for oneness with God?

God speaks to the soul

And God said to the soul:
    I desired you before the world began.
    I desire you now
    As you desire me.
    And where the desires of two come together
    There love is perfected.

(tr. by Oliver Davies)

How the soul
speaks to God

Lord, you are my lover,
My longing,
My flowing stream,
My sun,
And I am your reflection.

(tr. by Oliver Davies)

How God answers the soul

It is my nature that makes me love you often,
For I am love itself.

It is my longing that makes me love you intensely,
For I yearn to be loved from the heart.

It is my eternity that makes me love you long,
For I have no end.

(tr. by Oliver Davies)

The desert has many teachings

In the desert,
Turn toward emptiness,
Fleeing the self.

Stand alone,
Ask no one's help,
And your being will quiet,
Free from the bondage of things.

Those who cling to the world,
endeavor to free them;
Those who are free, praise.

Care for the sick,
But live alone,
Happy to drink from the waters of sorrow,
To kindle Love's fire
With the twigs of a simple life.

Thus you will live in the desert.

How God comes
to the soul

I descend on my love
As dew on a flower.

(tr. by Oliver Davies)

Effortlessly,
Love flows from God into man,
Like a bird
Who rivers the air
Without moving her wings.
Thus we move in His world,
One in body and soul,
Though outwardly separate in form.
As the Source strikes the note,
Humanity sings—
The Holy Spirit is our harpist,
And all strings
Which are touched in Love
Must sound.

God's absence

Ah blessed absence of God,
How lovingly I am bound to you!
You strengthen my will in its pain
And make dear to me
The long hard wait in my poor body.
The nearer I come to you,
The more wonderfully and abundantly
God comes upon me.
In pride, alas, I can easily lose you,
But in the depths of pure humility, O Lord,
I cannot fall away from you.
For the deeper I fall, the sweeter you taste.

(tr. by Oliver Davies)

True love in every moment praises God.
Longing love brings a sorrow sweet to the pure.
Seeking love belongs to itself alone.
Understanding love gives itself equally to all.
Enlightened love is mingled with the sadness of the world.
But selfless love bears an effortless fruit,
Working so quietly even the body cannot say how it comes and goes.

Of all that God has shown me
I can speak just the smallest word,
Not more than a honey bee
Takes on his foot
From an overspilling jar.

Marguerite Porete

(? – 1310)

Marguerite Porete is another example of a woman who found her path in the Beguine community of laywomen. In her Mirror of Simple Souls, *a mixture of poetry and prose composed over the ten-year period between 1285 and 1295, Marguerite wrote: "God has nowhere to put his goodness, if not in me . . . no place to put himself entire, if not in me. And by this means I am the exemplar of salvation, and what is more, I am the salvation itself of every creature, and the glory of God . . ." (tr. by Peter Dronke)*

Marguerite referred contemptuously to the established church as Sainte Eglise la Petite *("Little Holy Church"), and contrasted it to the "Great Holy Church" of enlightened souls "annihilated in God." Accused on the basis of her writings of the heresy of the Free Spirit (the belief that once the soul has reached maturity it is beyond both ordinary moral constraints and any need of the sacraments or Church to serve as intermediary between itself and God), Marguerite was publicly burned at the stake in Paris on June 1, 1310. During the year and a half that she was held in prison beforehand, she refused to say a word to her Inquisitor.*

Beloved, what do you want of me?
I contain all that was, and that is, and shall be,
I am filled with the all.
Take of me all you please—
if you want all of myself, I'll not say no.
Tell me, beloved, what you want of me—
I am Love, who am filled with the all:
what you want,
we want, beloved—
tell us your desire nakedly.

(tr. by Peter Dronke)

Hadewijch of Antwerp

(13th c.)

A Flemish Beguine about whom almost no facts are known, Hadewijch wrote of God and her mystical experience of the divine in terms of Love (Minne), a word grammatically feminine. She left a body of work consisting of poems in stanzas, poems in couplets, prose accounts of her visions, and a group of letters to several younger Beguine women for whom she served as "mistress," or spiritual guide. These writings, highly influential during the period immediately following her death, were then lost and only rediscovered by scholars in the nineteenth century amid a cache of medieval manuscripts found in Brussels.

Two excerpts from the letters make clear the nature of Hadewijch's teaching. Separated from her small community by threats of an accusation of heresy for the teaching of quietism, she grounded her advice to her charges in a compassionate trust in their own independent experience. In one letter, she counsels her reader (who, we may guess, has only recently undertaken the Beguine life of community and material simplicity) to make good use of whatever circumstances, positive or negative, come to her: "You have to consider by yourself how you endure what opposes you and how you are able to go without those things which are dear to you. Of all the things that can befall a young heart, this is truly the hardest one of all: going without what we like. And when something good befalls you, examine to what use you can put it, and how wise and how moderate you are with regard to it. Try and remain inwardly detached in all that happens to you: when you are troubled or when you enjoy peace of mind. And always contemplate the works of our Lord, for these can teach you perfection."

In another letter, Hadewijch wishes for her young friend her own mystical realization: "May God make known to you, dear child, who he is and how he treats his servants . . . how he consumes them within himself. From the depths of his wisdom, he shall teach you what he is and with what wonderful sweetness the one lover lives in the other and so permeates the other that they do not know themselves from each other. But they possess each other in mutual delight, mouth in mouth, heart in heart, body in body, soul in soul, while a single divine nature flows through them both and they both become one through each other, yet remaining always themselves. "(both letters tr. by Oliver Davies)

Love's maturity

In the beginning Love satisfies us.
When Love first spoke to me of love—
How I laughed at her in return!
But then she made me like the hazel trees,
Which blossom early in the season of darkness,
And bear fruit slowly.

(tr. by Oliver Davies)

Knowing Love in herself

I do not complain of suffering for Love,
It is right that I should always obey her,
For I can know her only as she is in herself,
Whether she commands in storm or in stillness.
This is a marvel beyond my understanding,
Which fills my whole heart
And makes me stray in a wild desert.

(tr. by Oliver Davies)

Love's constancy

Anyone who has waded
Through Love's turbulent waters,
Now feeling hunger and now satiety,
Is untouched by the season
Of withering or blooming,
For in the deepest
And most dangerous waters,
On the highest peaks,
Love is always the same.

(tr. by Oliver Davies)

The madness of love

The madness of love
Is a blessed fate;
And if we understood this
We would seek no other:
It brings into unity
What was divided,
And this is the truth:
Bitterness it makes sweet,
It makes the stranger a neighbor,
And what was lowly it raises on high.

(tr. by Oliver Davies)

Love has subjugated me:
To me this is no surprise,
For she is strong and I am weak.
She makes me
Unfree of myself,
Continually against my will.
She does with me what she wishes;
Nothing of myself remains to me;
Formerly I was rich,
Now I am poor: everything is lost in love.

(tr. by Mother Columba Hart)

Hadewijch II

(13th c.)

In the manuscript of Hadewijch's poetry, the first sixteen poems in couplets are followed by thirteen more in another hand, which most scholars believe to be also the work of another mind and temperament. The poems are more metaphysical and intellectual than those of Hadewijch I, and introduce a new vocabulary of words such as "plunge," "nakedness," and "overpassing," which would be drawn upon by later male mystics such as Ruysbroeck and Eckhart. Nothing is known of the author of these poems, but her work seems at times startlingly close to that of Buddhist and Hindu poets. The final excerpt given here, for example, could be as easily at home among the poems of Lal Ded (see pages 118–127), fitting in seamlessly in its directness, imagery, and meaning.

All things
are too small
to hold me,
I am so vast

In the Infinite
I reach
for the Uncreated

I have
touched it,
it undoes me
wider than wide

Everything else
is too narrow

You know this well,
you who are also there

If I desire something, I know it not,
For in a boundless unknowing
I have lost my very self.
In His mouth I am engulfed,
In a bottomless abyss;
Never could I come out of it.

as quoted by Jan van Ruysbroeck (1293–1381)

(tr. by Sheila Hughes)

Tighten
to nothing
the circle
that is
the world's things

Then the Naked
circle
can grow wide,
enlarging,
embracing all

You who want
knowledge,
seek the Oneness
within

There you
will find
the clear mirror
already waiting

The French Beguine

(late 13th c.)

The only fact known of the author of the "The Soul Speaks" is that she lived on the outskirts of the city of Lille at the end of the thirteenth century. This poet who speaks to us eerily as if from beyond the grave—perhaps because she was near death when she wrote, perhaps as a device to give authority to her expression and understanding—uses the imagery of common household life (as Pan Zhao did in "Needle and Thread" on page 28) to illuminate spiritual practice. Her idea that our difficulties and suffering should be seen not as hindrances or a simple sign of spiritual immaturity but as part of the process of the soul's transformation also appears in Anne Bradstreet's comment on page 149.

from The Soul Speaks

Beguines who hear these words,
If life on earth
Makes you weep and complain,
Find your comfort in God:
Know that it is His will
That keeps you dwelling here below,
And the more your hearts burn with love—
As mine did, when I lived—
The more lovely to Him you will be.
It is the color that He loves best,
The color in which He is clothed.
In this you will be like Him.

And if of some of you
He requires even more,
Asks of you a payment of pain,
Praise Him more joyously still:
The great Good that awaits you
Should make your patience strong.
As a rust-covered sword soon gleams
Beneath the weight of a polishing hand,
So the soul who gives herself truly
Comes to shine with the blows of God.

And just as we plunge pure wool
In the scarlet dye again and again,
To brighten and fix the color,
God transforms and guides the soul:
Difficulty and plunging grief
Will deepen its hue and its worth.
And if for love of your Creator
You can find patience in this sorrow,

You will surely receive the highest gift—
You will walk in glory and honor
In the vision of the Savior,
Having lived and burned for Him in human flesh.

(tr. by Jane Hirshfield with Samuel Michael Halevi)

Jusammi Chikako

(fl. ca. 1300)

Chikako "of the Third Rank," one of the leading poets of her time, served in the court of the Japanese Emperor Fushimi. Her poem is a vivid presentation of awakened mind: utterly independent of all the concerns and efforts of our conscious lives, it enters any door that is open to its shining presence. In fact, this poem implies, it may be easier for the bright moon (the symbol of enlightenment) to enter the house of human habitation when the inhabitants are not awake—not watching, or thinking, or hoping for some particular outcome. But still, the door must be left ajar. This is the state of mind of the shikantaza *meditation of Japanese Soto Zen: just being.*

On this summer night
All the household lies asleep,
    And in the doorway,
For once open after dark,
Stands the moon, brilliant, cloudless.

(tr. by Edwin A. Cranston)

Janabai

(1298?–1350?)

Born to a low-caste Indian family, from the age of seven Janabai was the household servant for the family of a renowned poet, Namadev. A member of the Varkari Sect, she wrote in Marathi, and is the most beloved of the bhakti women poets in that tradition. While other of her poems contain references to her Lord's keeping Janabai company while she performs her daily duties of sweeping and cleaning, the radical freedom from convention espoused in this poem resonates with many other works in this collection: whether by joining the strict forest community of Buddhist practitioners, by entering a Christian independent community of lay-women, or by wandering the marketplaces and forests of India in a state of ecstatic undress, some break with "ordinary" life is very often an important step in spiritual practice.

Cast off all shame,
and sell yourself
in the marketplace;
then alone
can you hope
to reach the Lord.

Cymbals in hand,
a *veena* upon my shoulder,
I go about;
who dares to stop me?

The *pallav* of my sari
falls away (A scandal!);
yet will I enter
the crowded marketplace
without a thought.

Jani says, My Lord,
I have become a slut
to reach Your home.

(tr. by Vilas Sarang)

veena: a stringed musical instrument; *pallav*: the end of the sari which goes over the shoulder

Catherine of Siena

(1347–1380)

The twenty-fourth of a family of twenty-five children, Saint Catherine was the daughter of Jacopo Benincasa, a cloth dyer in Siena. Determined from the age of six to devote her life solely to God, she became a novice in 1363 and a Dominican nun four years later. Catherine cared all her life for the poor and the ill, and in her later years also served as director to a group of nuns and as spiritual advisor to many laypeople from all stations in life. A social activist as well as a mystic, she was deeply engaged in the tumultuous religious politics of her time, even traveling to Avignon in an attempt to persuade the pope there to return to Rome. During her final illness (undoubtedly brought on by many years of "holy anorexia"), Catherine offered her physical suffering as a penance for the renewal of the Church, praying, "O eternal God, accept the sacrifice of my life within this mystic body of holy Church. I have nothing to give but what you have given me." (tr. by Suzanne Noffke, O.P.)

Although she left many letters as well as a treatise written for the nuns under her spiritual direction, Catherine was illiterate for most of her life, and her prayers were recorded by those who were present when she spoke them. She often entered into an ecstatic trance state before or during the course of her meditations, sometimes lying immobile on the ground, at other times kneeling or walking; her words would come in brief bursts interrupted by long periods of intense silence. During more peaceful times, she could be overheard singing her devotions as she walked alone in the convent's garden. The prayer given here dates from near the end of her life.

from Prayer 20

We were enclosed,
O eternal Father,
within the garden of your breast.
You drew us out of your holy mind
like a flower
petaled with our soul's three powers,
and into each power
you put the whole plant,
so that they might bear fruit in your garden,
might come back to you
with the fruit you gave them.
And you would come back to the soul,
to fill her with your blessedness.
There the soul dwells—
like the fish in the sea
and the sea in the fish.

(tr. by Suzanne Noffke, O.P.)

Lal Ded

(14th c.?)

Also known as Lalleswari, Lalla, or Lal Diddi, Lal Ded was born in Kashmir. Married at the age of twelve, she was neglected by her husband and treated harshly by her mother-in-law; after twelve years she left their house to become a disciple in the Shiva-worship tradition of oneness between God and the phenomenal world. Her words show both the unmistakable clarity and the joy of her experience of that union.

After completing her training, Lal Ded wandered the countryside in a state of undress, singing and dancing her passionate mystical experience. One story about her: One morning, after a group of children taunted the wandering devotee, a cloth merchant came spiritedly to her defense. She immediately purchased two bundles of cloth of equal weight from him and continued on her way. As she went through the day, each time someone ridiculed her, she tied a knot in the cloth on her left shoulder; each time someone praised her, she tied a knot in the cloth on the right. At day's end, she returned to the merchant, and asked him to weigh the bundles again. She thanked him for his earlier concern, but also pointed out that, as he could see for himself, nothing had changed: whatever praise or blame she received, they were of equal weight, and she accepted both with the same attitude of equanimity.

I drag a boat over the ocean
with a solid rope.
Will God hear?
Will he take me all the way?
Like water in goblets of unbaked clay
I drip out slowly,
and dry.
My soul whirls. Dizzy. Let me
discover my home.

(tr. by Willis Barnstone)

I was passionate,
filled with longing,
I searched
far and wide.

But the day
that the Truthful One
found me,
I was at home.

The soul, like the moon,
is new, and always new again.

And I have seen the ocean
continuously creating.

Since I scoured my mind
and my body, I too, Lalla,
am new, each moment new.

My teacher told me one thing,
Live in the soul.

When that was so,
I began to go naked,
and dance.

(*tr. by Coleman Barks*)

This world,
compared to You—

a lake so tiny
even a mustard seed
is too large for it to hold.

Yet from that lake all Beings drink.

And into it deer, jackals,
rhinoceri, sea-elephants falling.

From the earliest moment of birth,
falling and falling
in You.

Coursing in emptiness,
I, Lalla,
dropped off body and mind,

and stepped into the Secret Self.

Look: Lalla the sedgeflower
blossomed a lotus.

To learn the scriptures is easy,
to live them, hard.
The search for the Real
is no simple matter.

Deep in my looking,
the last words vanished.
Joyous and silent,
the waking that met me there.

I searched for my Self
until I grew weary,

but no one, I know now,
reaches the hidden knowledge
by means of effort.

Then, absorbed in "Thou art This,"
I found the place of Wine.

There all the jars are filled,
but no one is left to drink.

On the way to God the difficulties
feel like being ground by a millstone,
like night coming at noon, like
lightning through the clouds.

But don't worry!
What must come, comes.
Face everything with love,
as your mind dissolves in God.

(tr. by Coleman Barks)

At the end of a crazy-moon night
the love of God rose.
I said, "It's me, Lalla."

The Beloved woke. We became That,
and the lake is crystal-clear.

(tr. by Coleman Barks)

Vittoria Colonna

(1492–1547)

Born in 1492 to a family of Roman nobility, Vittoria Colonna was betrothed at the age of three to a Neapolitan prince whom she married when she was seventeen. One year later, he embarked on a career in the military, and afterward returned home only rarely until his death in battle in 1525. Though she had no children of her own, Colonna raised an orphaned cousin of her husband's. By her twenties she was established as one of the major literary figures of her time; among her friends were such poets and churchmen as Bembo, Ariosto, Bernardo Tasso, and Castiglione, each of whom praised her poetic eloquence, virtue, and beauty.

After she became a widow, Colonna entered the Convent of San Silvestro in Rome as a lay resident. Although she never took formal vows, for the rest of her life she made her home in various convents, devoting herself to prayer and contemplation, and also involving herself actively in the movement to reform the church. From the 1530s until her death in 1547, Colonna's closest spiritual friend was Michelangelo. The two exchanged letters and poems, Michelangelo gave Colonna numerous drawings, and they saw each other frequently. In one poem addressed to her, the artist said, "the nearer I am to you, the less my soul knows of fear"; in a letter, he wrote, "I wish to do more for you than for anyone else I have known on earth." Although Colonna's love poetry was written first and is better known today, her collected works include 217 spiritual sonnets.

As a starved little bird, who sees and hears
his mother's wings fluttering round about him
To bring him food, whose heart is filled with love
Both for her and the food, who then, rejoicing
—Though in the nest he pines and is consumed
With eagerness to follow her and fly—
Will thank her by his singing, far beyond
His usual power of song, with tongue set free,
So I, whenever the warm living rays
Of the divine Sun, nourishing my heart,
Will shine on me with unaccustomed brightness,
Take up my pen, impelled by inner love;
Without quite knowing what it is I say,
As best I can, I write His praises down.

(tr. by Laura Anna Stortoni and Mary Prentice Lillie)

I see in my mind, surrounding God,
in the form of a mosaic, a high wall
of living sparks, winged and quick,
so well interwoven with love's chains
    that each one offers to the others pure light
without any shadow to make bright and dark,
but living splendor of the heavenly Sun
which adorns, colors, arranges, and clothes them;
    and then I see Her, whom, still in human form,
heaven honors with a glory second only
to the true radiance of the Son, and the primal Light,
    whose beauty a living mind can never
hope to draw with paint or with words,
or poetry approach with sufficient praise.

(tr. by Samuel Michael Halevi)

Mirabai

(1498–1565?)

Mirabai, the most famous of all the northern Indian women bhakti *poets, was educated in literature and music by tutors in the court of her grandfather, Rao Dudaji, a man known for his piety. She married the crown prince of Mewar, but, like Mahadeviyakka three centuries before, soon came to reject any husband but her Lord—in Mirabai's case, Giridhara, a manifestation of Shiva known for the miraculous lifting of a mountain. There are legends that Mirabai's husband's family tried twice to kill her, and also that she refused to throw herself on his funeral pyre upon his death. Whatever the facts, it is clear from her poems that she eventually took up the wandering life familiar to us from earlier women Shiva devotees, turning her back on convention and finding her only joy in a passionate dedication to her Lord Giridhara. She spent her final years at the temple compound of Ranachora at Dvarka. To this day, her poems are widely sung throughout the Indian subcontinent, often in different versions, depending on the religious tradition of the singer.*

Reading through the body of Mirabai's work gives us a poignant picture of both the passion of mystical union and the despair of longing for a union once experienced but now missed—a longing so strong that it becomes in itself the sign of the Beloved's presence. This theme is visible elsewhere in this book as well, but in Mirabai's songs the two states at times shift one into the other with the blurring speed of a hummingbird's wings: she declares her Lord's presence within her in one moment, and begs him to allow her to be with him the next.

Along with the first piece given here, other poems in this book that deal with the experience of fulfillment's departure are Mechtild of Magdeburg's "God's absence" (page 94) and Nelly Sachs's "But perhaps God needs the longing" (page 224). Such poems remind us that even a powerful mystical opening does not necessarily guarantee serenity. The dark night of the soul can follow the knowledge of union as well as precede it—as the Bible also shows, when even such a figure as Jesus is depicted as being subject to the sense of utter abandonment. But as we have already seen in poems by Izumi Shikibu and Mahadeviyakka, it may be that it is through our vulnerability itself that the always-present sacred can make itself known; and for some, a time does come when that knowledge becomes utterly unshakable: seamless, illimitable, and beyond question. Whether or not such a moment arrived for Mirabai, we cannot know.

O friends, I am mad
with love, and no one sees.

My mattress is a sword-point,
how can I sleep
when the bed of my Beloved
is spread open elsewhere?

Only those who have felt the knife
can understand the wound,
only the jeweler
knows the nature of the Jewel.

I have lost it,
and though anguish takes me door to door,
no doctor answers.

Mira calls her Lord: O Dark One,
Only You can heal this pain.

Love has stained my body
to the color of the One Who Holds Up Mountains.
When I dressed in the world's five fabrics,
I only played hide and seek—
For disguised though I was, the Lifting One caught me.
And seeing his beauty, I offered him all that I am.
Friends, let those whose Beloved is absent write letters—
Mine dwells in the heart, and neither enters nor leaves.
Mira has given herself to her Lord Giridhara.
Day or night, she serves only Him.

All I Was Doing Was Breathing

Something has reached out and taken in the beams of my eyes.
There is a longing, it is for his body, for every hair of that dark body.
All I was doing was being, and the Dancing Energy came by my
     house.
His face looks curiously like the moon, I saw it from the side,
     smiling.
My family says: "Don't ever see him again!" And implies things in a
     low voice.
But my eyes have their own life; they laugh at rules, and know whose
     they are.
I believe I can bear on my shoulders whatever you want to say of me.
Mira says: Without the energy that lifts mountains, how am I to
     live?

(tr. by Robert Bly)

The wild woman of the forests
Discovered the sweet plums by tasting,
And brought them to her Lord—
She who was neither cultured nor lovely,
She who was filthy in disarrayed clothes,
She of the lowest of castes.
But the Lord, seeing her heart,
Took the ruined plums from her hand.
She saw no difference between low and high,
Wanting only the milk of his presence.
Illiterate, she never studied the Teachings—
A single turn of the chariot's wheel
Brought her to Knowledge.
Now she is bound to the Storm Bodied One
By gold cords of Love, and wanders *his* woods.
Servant Mira says:
Whoever can love like this will be saved.
My Master lifts all that is fallen,
And from the beginning I have been the handmaiden
Herding cows by his side.

O friends on this Path,
My eyes are no longer my eyes.
A sweetness has entered through them,
Has pierced through to my heart.
For how long did I stand in the house of this body
And stare at the road?
My Beloved is a steeped herb, he has cured me for life.
Mira belongs to Giridhara, the One who lifts all,
And everyone says she is mad.

The song of the flute, O sister, is madness.
I thought that nothing that was not God could hold me,
But hearing that sound, I lose mind and body,
My heart wholly caught in the net.
O flute, what were your vows, what is your practice?
What power sits by your side?
Even Mira's Lord is trapped in Your seven notes.

O friend, understand: the body
is like the ocean,
rich with hidden treasures.

Open your inmost chamber and light its lamp.

Within the body are gardens,
rare flowers, peacocks, the inner Music;
within the body a lake of bliss,
on it the white soul-swans take their joy.

And in the body, a vast market—
go there, trade,
sell yourself for a profit you can't spend.

Mira says, her Lord is beyond praising.
Allow her to dwell near Your feet.

Why Mira Can't Go Back to Her Old House

The colors of the Dark One have penetrated Mira's body; all the
 other colors washed out.
Making love with the Dark One and eating little, those are my pearls
 and my carnelians.
Meditation beads and the forehead streak, those are my scarves and
 my rings.
That's enough feminine wiles for me. My teacher taught me this.
Approve me or disapprove me: I praise the Mountain Energy night
 and day.
I take the path that ecstatic human beings have taken for centuries.
I don't steal money, I don't hit anyone. What will you charge me
 with?
I have felt the swaying of the elephant's shoulders; and now you want
 me to climb on a jackass? Try to be serious.

(tr. by Robert Bly)

I was going to the river for water,
the gold pitcher balanced with care upon my head,
and Love's knife entered my heart.
Now God has bound me tightly with that fine thread,
he takes me wherever he will.
Mira's Lord is the dark–bodied, beautiful Giridhara.
What he wishes to be, he is.

The Heat of Midnight Tears

Listen, my friend, this road is the heart opening,
kissing his feet, resistance broken, tears all night.

If we could reach the Lord through immersion in water,
I would have asked to be born a fish in this life.
If we could reach Him through nothing but berries and wild nuts
then surely the saints would have been monkeys when they came
     from the womb!
If we could reach him by munching lettuce and dry leaves
then the goats would surely get to the Holy One before us!

If the worship of stone statues could bring us all the way,
I would have adored a granite mountain years ago.

Mirabai says, "The heat of midnight tears will bring you to God."

(tr. by Robert Bly)

It's True I Went to the Market

My friend, I went to the market and bought the Dark One.
You claim by night, I claim by day.
Actually I was beating a drum all the time I was buying him.
You say I gave too much; I say too little.
Actually, I put him on a scale before I bought him.
What I paid was my social body, my town body, my family body, and
    all my inherited jewels.
Mirabai says: The Dark One is my husband now.
Be with me when I lie down; you promised me this in an earlier life.

(tr. by Robert Bly)

Teresa of Avila

(1515–1582)

Teresa de Cepeda y Ahumada was born into a noble Spanish family on March 28, 1515, one of a dozen children. Although she had sometimes played at religious life as a child, when she was sent at age thirteen to a convent boarding school, after the death of her mother, she did not care for the life she found there. Only thoughts of death and hell (brought on by a serious illness) caused her to change her mind, and, in her own words, "in servile fear" she "forced herself" to embrace the cloister in 1536. Yet immediately afterward, she wrote, "there came to me a new joy, which amazed me, for I could not understand whence it came." (this and the following tr. by E. Allison Peers)

For twenty years, Teresa struggled with ill health and the rigors of spiritual discipline as she pursued contemplative prayer, using a Franciscan book as her only guide in a Carmelite order that did not stress the contemplative life. In 1555, she experienced what she called a second conversion: "I could not possibly doubt that He was within me or that I was wholly engulfed in Him." At that time she also began to receive regular visions "with the eyes of the soul" and to hear the inner voice of God's wishes for her life.

Influenced by these visions, Teresa determined to found a small convent within the new Discalced ("unshod"; that is, sandal-wearing) movement for reform among Carmelite monastics. The movement's call for a return to "holy poverty" meant that the new religious house would not be endowed but would survive only on alms, and this created a storm of opposition both within the religious community and from local authorities. In the end, though, Teresa could not be stopped, and in 1563 she and a handful of sisters moved into the tiny convent of St. Joseph's.

For the next twenty-five years Teresa continued to expand her reform movement, traveling over rough roads in an open wooden cart to establish new religious houses throughout Spain. She wrote a number of books for the guidance of her followers, including the Life *(an autobiography that contains a much-loved treatise on the four stages of prayer),* The Way of Perfection, *and* The Interior Castle. *The young St. John of the Cross was the first priest to enter the Reformed mon-*

*astery she opened for men, and later became the confessor for one of her commu-
nities; the spiritual friendship of the two Carmelites is legendary.*

*Called a saint even during her lifetime, Teresa was nonetheless the most hu-
man of saints. She had a keen sense of humor, and continually teased and laughed
with her companions. She worked hard at scrubbing and cleaning each new house
that she opened, and emphasized that there were other paths to God besides the
contemplative: "Remember that there must be someone to cook the meals, and
count yourselves happy in being able to serve like Martha," she told her nuns, and
added, "the Lord walks among pots and pans."*

*Teresa's letters and autobiography show that she was given to despair as well as
joy, and to ordinary loneliness as well as mystical union. (She was known, though,
to dislike "gloomy people," and in one of her prayers asked that she be delivered
from "frowning saints.") Earlier in her life, she wrote a poem with the refrain "I
die because I do not die," expressing her eagerness to leave this world for a higher
one, but in her full maturity even this longing fell away—perfection, she now felt,
was the life she was given as much as any future one in Heaven. She died in 1582,
while traveling back to her beloved Avila after opening the seventeenth house of
her order.*

(Lines written on a bookmark found in her Breviary)

Let nothing disturb thee,
Nothing affright thee;
All things are passing;
God never changeth;
Patient endurance
Attaineth to all things;
Who God possesseth
In nothing is wanting;
Alone God sufficeth.

(tr. by Henry Wadsworth Longfellow)

Maria de' Medici, Queen of France

(1573–1642)

Maria de' Medici was born in Florence and raised in the Medici tradition of humanism and support for the arts. In 1600 she became Henry IV of France's second wife. Following his death she was made regent for their son, Louis XIII, but after Louis came of age, he quarreled with his mother, ordering her confined against her will; she also earned the enmity of the powerful Cardinal Richelieu. The result was that from 1631 until her death eleven years later, Maria lived in exile.

(To the Virgin)

Let not my titles, crowns, and worldly honors
Cause me to glory in my rank and beauty—
Emperors are thy servants, as are kings.
I am a queen myself—and thy handmaiden.
All who would honor me should call me so.
O let my only glory be thy service!
Thou art the Queen of the Eternal Light.
We mortals reign but over dreams and shadows.

(tr. by Laura Anna Stortoni and Mary Prentice Lillie)

Two Nahuatl Invocations

(early 1600s)

In 1629, Hernando Ruiz de Alarcón, a Catholic parish priest, completed his decade-long project of compiling a "Treatise on the Superstitions and Heathen Customs That Today Live Among the Indians Native to This New Spain"—a work intended to serve the Church in recognizing and prosecuting those Indians who continued to hold native Mesoamerican beliefs. Despite the behavior stemming from his religious position, however, Ruiz cared genuinely about the well-being of the native population, not just their souls: he was one of very few priests to become fluent in Nahuatl, and he actively protested the extermination of the Indian people occurring all around him, blaming it on the inadequacies of Church policies. Ironically, the one surviving manuscript of his work is now the primary source by which the details of the everyday practices of the indigenous religion of that time are known.

Ruiz recorded the words of midwives (invariably female) and of ticitl—sorcerers, diviners, and healers—of whom he wrote, "I have seized and punished many Indian men and women for this transgression, and I have calculated that there have been more women than men." Among women the "Treatise" names were Catalina Paula, Magdalena Petronilla Xochiquetzal, and Marta Monica, the wife of a mayor. Some invocations and spells were handed down, others came to the women in moments of ecstatic knowledge, often prompted by hallucinogens, either morning glory seeds or peyote.

Many chants begin with the phrase that opens the first one given here: "I myself, Spirit in Flesh." The poet and translator Francisco X. Alarcón (who may be a descendent of Ruiz) tells us that this phrase functions as a kind of magical "abracadabra," opening the door between human and spirit worlds. The sorceress, in pronouncing them, enters into oneness with and speaks in the voice of the invoked god. In the second chant we see the idea that within objects as well a sacred presence waits to be called forth.

Belief that human and spirit realities meet on earth runs throughout Ruiz's record. At the start of the "Treatise" he writes, "Almost all present-day forms of worship . . . have their roots and formal basis in [the Indians'] belief that the clouds are angels and gods worthy of worship. They think the same of the winds, since they believe these forces live everywhere, in the hills, mountains, valleys, and ravines. They believe the same of the rivers, lakes, and springs, since they offer wax and incense to all the above." (tr. by Francisco X. Alarcón)

(Invocation for storing corn)

I myself
Spirit in Flesh:

come forth
elder sister
Lady of Our Flesh

soon I shall place you
inside my jade jar

hold up the four directions
don't shame yourself

you shall be my breath
you shall be my cure

for me, Poor Orphan
for me, Centeotl

you, my elder sister
you, Tonacacihuatl

(tr. by Francisco X. Alarcón)

Poor Orphan: one of the metaphorical names for Tezcatlipoca (Smoking Mirror), the dual-natured god of sorcerers; *Centeotl*: Ear-of-Corn God; *Tonacacihuatl*: Lady of Our Flesh, goddess of corn

(A midwife's invocation)

*After [a woman] has given birth, the [ritual] with
the newborn then begins. To wash it, they cast a spell
on the vessel and on the water, thus:*

Please come forth,
My jade calabash-cup
And my mother Jade-skirted One;
Soon you will bathe here,
Soon you will cleanse here
What was born in your hands,
What came to life in your hands.

(*tr. by Michael D. Coe and Gordon Whittaker*)

my mother Jade-skirted One: goddess of water

Anne Bradstreet

(1612–1672)

The first writer of either sex in colonial America to publish a book of poems, Anne Bradstreet was born in England and came to Massachusetts at the age of eighteen on the Arbella, *along with Simon Bradstreet, her husband of two years, and her parents. Her father became the second governor of the colony; later, her husband held the office as well. Anne eventually gave birth to eight children, and her poems offer us a portrait of a marriage of both mutual devotion and passion. They also show us a woman of wide curiosity and learning who took up such fundamental Puritan subjects as the ultimate emptiness of worldly existence and the acceptance of God's will in encountering the vicissitudes of personal life.*

Whether dealing with the death of a grandchild, the loss of her home to fire, illness, or the absence of her husband, Bradstreet sought meaning within the context of her religion. She described her outlook in "Meditations Divine and Moral," a collection of thoughts written down for one of her sons: "There is no object that we see, no action that we do, no good that we enjoy, no evil that we feel or fear, but we may make some spiritual advantage of all." This woman whose life was filled with cause for sorrow also wrote, "Downy beds make drowsy persons, but hard lodging keeps the eyes open; a prosperous state makes a secure Christian, but adversity makes him consider."

from The Vanity of All Worldly Things

There is a path no vulture's eye hath seen,
Where lion fierce, nor lion's whelps have been,
Which leads unto that living crystal fount,
Who drinks thereof, the world doth nought account.
The depth and sea have said " 'tis not in me,"
With pearl and gold it shall not valued be.
For sapphire, onyx, topaz who would change;
It's hid from eyes of men, they count it strange.
Death and destruction the fame hath heard,
But where and what it is, from heaven's declared;
It brings to honour which shall ne'er decay,
It stores with wealth which time can't wear away.
It yieldeth pleasures far beyond conceit,
And truly beautifies without deceit.
Nor strength, nor wisdom, nor fresh youth shall fade,
Nor death shall see, but are immortal made.
This pearl of price, this tree of life, this spring,
Who is possessed of shall reign a king.
Nor change of state nor cares shall ever see,
But wear his crown unto eternity.
This satiates the soul, this stays the mind,
And all the rest, but vanity we find.

Catharina Regina von Greiffenberg

(1633–1694)

Catharina Regina von Greiffenberg was born in 1633 to a family of Austrian Protestant nobility and educated by an uncle whom she married when she was thirty-one. Active in the struggle between Protestantism and Catholicism, Catharina wrote many letters in the service of her beliefs, and her collection of spiritual sonnets is considered the greatest work by a woman writer of the German High Baroque. Her poetry, densely textured and highly worked, echoes the overflowing world of nature's richness that she considered a mirror and receptacle for the glory of the divine presence.

On the Ineffable Inspiration of the Holy Spirit

You unseen lightning flash, you darkly radiant light,
you power that's heart-infused, incomprehensible being!
Something divine within my spirit had its being
That stirs and spurs me: I sense a curious light.

Never by its own power the soul is thus alight.
It was a miracle-wind, a spirit, a creative being,
The eternal power of breath, prime origin of being
That in me kindled for himself this heaven-flaring light.

You mirror-spectrum-glance, you many-colored gleam!
You glitter to and fro, are incomprehensibly clear;
in truth's own sunlight the spirit-dove-flights gleam.

The God-stirred pool has also been troubled clear!
First on the spirit-sun reflecting it casts its gleam,
The moon; then turns about, and earthward, too, is clear.

(tr. by Michael Hamburger)

On the Fruit-Providing Autumn Season

Joy-fulfiller/fruit provider/many-skilled cook of the whole year/
Verdure's bloom, time's consummation/toil-inspired relish-need!
Drawn-out hope/in you has proved itself, to rest in you made speed.
Without you there is looking only/no full enjoyment here.
Perfection of the seasons, now make perfect sheer
what by the power of flowering, growth to half-life could proceed.
Your working alone can glory in the labor done indeed.
Precious season-treasure, so high now drive that blossoming's
    cheer/
from your rich cornucopia pour long-hoped-for joy's fruition.
Sweet lovable mouth-delighter, our spirits refresh as well:
thus in conjunction these he'll elevate to praise-emission.
Season with that the longed-for season where sovereign orders
    dwell.
Let seminal pips turn black, with juice the Providence-apples cloy
so that God's fruits of grace on earth we eat and, savoring, enjoy.

(tr. by Michael Hamburger)

from On the Sweet Comfort
Brought by Grace

I look
at gold and world
and see
children's trinkets and sand.
Heaven-joy carries me
far beyond my self.

If only my breath
were a wind
through-sweetened with praise,
to carry Love's flames
starwards, toward You.

If only I,
out of Love,
could be the phoenix kindled,
could perish entirely out of bliss,
into my one desire.

Let me in thankfulness
be Your mirror,
God—
Then Your own rays
might be returned to You,
in grace-words, in equal light.

(tr. by Jane Hirshfield
with Samuel Michael Halevi)

Sor Juana Inés de la Cruz

(1648?–1695)

One of the foremost writers of Spanish literature, Juana Ramirez de Asbaje was born in San Miguel Nepantla, in New Spain (Mexico), in 1648 or 1651. Her mother, Isabel Ramirez , was illiterate, and did not marry either Juana's Basque father or another man to whom she later bore three children, yet she managed a large hacienda whose leasehold she had inherited from her father and looked after the welfare of her children assiduously.

Juana learned to read at the age of three by telling her elder sister's tutor that she had also been sent to the lessons by her mother. She immediately began exploring the shelves of her grandfather's library, and by the time she was five or six the exceptional nature of her intelligence was clear. At one point she asked her mother if she might not disguise herself as a man in order to attend the university; at another, she cut off her hair until she had mastered a particularly difficult lesson, proclaiming that a head devoid of learning should not be adorned with vanity.

Isabel sent her daughter at the age of eight to live with an aunt in Mexico City, and when Juana turned fifteen she joined the court of the Viceroy and Vicereine of New Spain as a lady-in-waiting. There, Juana astonished everyone with her learning, including a panel of forty prominent men of letters assembled one day to test her. The Viceroy described her performance as resembling that of a "great galleon under attack by a few small canoes."

At twenty, Juana became a nun in the convent of San Jeronimo. In a letter addressed years later to her Bishop, she explained this decision in less than entirely spiritual terms: "Given the total antipathy I felt toward marriage, I deemed convent life the least unsuitable and the most honorable I could elect if I were to ensure my salvation." (tr. by Margaret Sayers Peden) From her cell—more accurately a suite of private rooms—Juana continued to play a central part in the intellectual life of her times: she pursued her studies, read and corresponded widely, undertook scientific experiments, even designed a triumphal arch to welcome a new Viceroy to the capital. While nuns could not leave the convent, they received visitors freely, and Sor Juana became a favorite of several succeeding Vicereines.

Juana's subject of investigation was knowledge itself, all knowledge, and she wrote hundreds of poems that were primarily secular in nature as well as lyrics for the convent's religious plays, verses for public festivals (of which the two poems given here are examples), and a theological essay. The freedom of her thinking did not escape the attention of Church authorities. After more than twenty years of convent life, a crisis arose: shortly after the recipient published a letter of Juana's in which she defended not only her own interest in worldly learning but also the broad rights of women to education and a life of the mind, power shifted away from her protectors at court and into the hands of churchmen who had long disapproved of her. Subjected to a lengthy firestorm of criticism, and aware of the vulnerable nature of her position as a nun, Juana finally obeyed the archbishop who had determined to achieve her salvation—a man who thanked God for making him nearsighted so that he would not be able to see women. After a confession which lasted several weeks, she signed with her own blood a new profession of faith, and was stripped of all her possessions (including her beloved library of over 4,000 volumes), which were immediately sold for the benefit of the poor. She then undertook a life of prayer, silence, and severe physical penance. Two years later, she died of an epidemic that swept through the convent.

It is interesting to compare Sor Juana's life and fate with those of other women in this book. Vittoria Colonna and Izumi Shikibu, for example, were also remarkably intelligent women who began their adult lives in a court milieu. Given the freedom to explore their interests on their own, they turned with gratitude to monastic life for contemplation and shelter, but did not bind themselves to it by formal vows. Many other women found in these pages chose joyously to devote their lives wholly to spiritual practice. Juana Ramirez , however, was driven into the convent because she saw no other viable way of life for a woman of her type in her culture; though she was undoubtedly a true believer, her marriage vows to Christ became in the end, for her, a prison. We have no way of knowing her experience during her final two years, as she was forbidden all writing. One can only hope that her innate courage served her in this last stage of her life as well as it had served her before.

from the fifth *villancico, in*
alternating voices, written for the
Feast of the Nativity in Puebla, 1689

Because my Lord was born to suffer,
let Him stay awake.

    Because for me He is awake,
    let Him fall asleep.

Let Him stay awake—
there is no pain for one who loves
as painlessness would be.

    Let Him sleep—
    for one who sleeps, in dreaming,
    prepares himself to die.

Silence, now He sleeps!
    Careful, He's awake!
Do not disturb Him, no!
    Yes, He must be waked!
Let Him wake and wake!
    Let Him have his sleep!

villancico: a poetic form derived from the simple language and strong rhythms of peasant
songs, written to be part of the great religious festival celebrations held in cities throughout
New Spain

from the first *villancico*,
written for the Nativity of
Our Lord, Puebla, 1689

    Since Love is shivering
in the ice and cold,
since hoarfrost and snow
have ringed him round,
who will come to his aid?
   Water!
      Earth!
         Air!
No, Fire will!
    Since the Child is assailed
by pains and ills
and has no breath left
to face his woes,
who will come to his aid?
   Fire!
      Earth!
         Water!
No, but Air will!
    Since the loving Child
is burning hot,
that he breathes a volcanic
deluge of flame,
who will come to his aid?
   Air!
      Fire!
         Earth!
No, Water will!
    Since today the Child
leaves heaven for earth
and finds nowhere to rest
his head in this world,

who will come to his aid?
Water!
Fire!
Air!
No, but Earth will!

(tr. by Alan S. Trueblood)

Chiyō-ni

(1703–1775)

Kaga no Chiyō, considered one of the foremost women haiku poets, began writing at the age of seven. She studied under two haiku masters who had themselves apprenticed with the great poet Bashō. It is not known if Chiyō ever married, though one poem often attributed to her speaks of the death of a young son. In 1755, Chiyō became a Buddhist nun—not, she said, in order to renounce the world, but as a way "to teach her heart to be like the clear water which flows night and day."

In the early American Buddhist publication The Way, *D. T. Suzuki wrote at length about the first haiku presented here, one of Chiyō's most famous, which he translated,* Oh, morning glory!/The bucket taken captive,/Water begged for. *"The idea is this: One summer morning Chiyō the poetess got up early wishing to draw water from the well . . . She found the bucket entwined by the blooming morning glory vine. She was so struck . . . that she forgot all about her business and stood before it thoroughly absorbed in contemplation. The only words she could utter were 'Oh, the morning glory!' At the time, the poetess was not conscious of herself or of the morning glory as standing against [outside] her. Her mind was filled with the flower, the whole world turned into the flower, she was the flower itself. . .*

"The first line, 'Oh, morning glory!' does not contain anything intellectual . . . it is the feeling, pure and simple, and we may interpret it in any way we like. The following two lines, however, determine the nature and depth of what was in the mind of the poetess: when she tells us about going to the neighbor for water we know that she just left the morning glory as she found it . . . she does not even dare touch the flower, much less pluck it, for in her inmost consciousness there is the feeling that she is perfectly one with reality. . . .

"When beauty is expressed in terms of Buddhism, it is a form of self-enjoyment of the suchness of things. Flowers are flowers, mountains are mountains, I sit here, you stand there, and the world goes on from eternity to eternity; this is the suchness of things."

The morning glory!
It has taken the well bucket,
I must ask elsewhere for water.

(tr. by Robert Aitken)

Grazing
my fishing line—
the summer moon.

(tr. by Jane Hirshfield, Michael Katz,
and Mariko Aratani)

From the mind
of a single, long vine,
one hundred opening lives.

*(tr. by Jane Hirshfield
and Mariko Aratani)*

Ann Griffiths

(1776–1805)

One of the verse forms most practiced by women of the eighteenth and nineteenth centuries was the writing of hymns. This considerable body of work is represented in this book with a hymn by Ann Griffiths, a Methodist mystic considered the greatest woman poet of the Welsh language.

Born Nansi (Ann) Thomas, Griffiths was the daughter of a tenant farmer in the district of Berwyns, Wales. Her family's faith was originally Church of England, and their attendance at the nearby parish church was so reliable that on the rare occasions when they failed to attend because of illness, the family dog could still be found in his usual place outside the church door. Ann learned to read and write over the course of three years' study with a neighboring woman, and in her part of Wales the composing of verses and singing of carols was a common activity during long winter nights spent knitting stockings by the fire.

The elder of Ann's two brothers was the first of the family to be swept up in the evangelical Methodist movement that occurred during the 1790s in Wales, and the rest of the family soon followed. In 1796, after hearing the sermon of a visiting preacher, Ann was converted, and she quickly became deeply involved in her new community: inviting itinerant preachers to dinner, corresponding with fellow converts, and traveling many miles to attend Communion monthly. She also began to experience moments of "visitation" in which she might burst into tears, or, conversely, fall into a state of deep exultation. She was at times discovered standing in the kitchen in a complete trance, or she might step outside the back door to the nearby shed for a few potatoes, only to be found there, much later, utterly absorbed. Shortly after her father's death in 1804, Ann married a neighboring farmer, Thomas Griffiths. A year later, two weeks after giving birth to a child who lived only a few minutes, she also died.

The body of Ann Griffiths's work consists of thirty-four brief hymns, which were not written down until after her death, and a handful of letters. The hymn given here takes its imagery from the Old Testament "Song of Songs" (see the last three lines on page 24, a motif repeated throughout the "Songs"), but the circum-

stances of that poem have been altered: the Beloved is now clearly Christ, and it is not "love" which must not be awakened "until it is ripe," but the Divine Presence himself—a theme which, though handled quite differently, can also be seen in the festive villancico *of Sor Juana found on page 157.*

H is left hand, in heat of noonday,
Lovingly my head upholds,
And his right hand, filled with blessings,
Tenderly my soul enfolds.
I adjure you, nature's darlings,
Beautiful in field and grove,
Stir not up, till he be willing,
Him who is my glorious Love.

(tr. by H. A. Hodges)

Emily Brontë

(1818–1848)

Emily Brontë was one of six children born into the household of Patrick Brontë, a clergyman. Her mother died early in Emily's childhood, after which her father's sister came to care for the young family. Following the deaths of two older sisters during an epidemic, the remaining children (Charlotte, Emily, Branwell, and Anne) were educated at home. They soon developed an intricate life of the imagination, creating a mythical kingdom, Gondal, for which they wrote stories and plays.

Emily left home briefly, preparing for a career in teaching, but the death of her aunt allowed her what she most desired: to return to the parsonage at Haworth, where she could walk the moors, keep house for her father, and pursue her writing in the company of her siblings. In 1848, Emily nursed her brother through his final illness, brought on by opium addiction and drinking. She developed what seemed like a cold the day of his funeral, refused to take to her bed or see a doctor, and two months later died of consumption at the age of thirty.

In 1846, after Charlotte had "stumbled upon" Emily's poems and found them extraordinarily moving, the three sisters published a joint volume of their verse under the pseudonyms Currer, Ellis, and Acton Bell (names of deliberately ambiguous gender). The book did not do well, but each of the sisters nonetheless went on to write and publish novels; Emily's, of course, was Wuthering Heights.

Charlotte Brontë reported that the untitled poem given here contains the last lines Emily ever wrote.

No coward soul is mine,
No trembler in the world's storm-troubled sphere:
I see Heaven's glories shine,
And faith shines equal, arming me from fear.

O God within my breast,
Almighty, ever-present Deity!
Life—that in me has rest,
As I—undying Life—have power in Thee!

Vain are the thousand creeds
That move men's hearts: unutterably vain;
Worthless as withered weeds,
Or idlest froth amid the boundless main,

To waken doubt in one
Holding so fast by Thine infinity;
So surely anchored on
The steadfast rock of immortality.

With wide-embracing love
Thy spirit animates eternal years,
Pervades and broods above,
Changes, sustains, dissolves, creates, and rears.

Though earth and man were gone,
And suns and universes ceased to be,
And Thou were left alone,
Every existence would exist in Thee.

There is not room for Death,
nor atom that his might could render void:
Thou—thou art Being and Breath,
And what thou art may never be destroyed.

Bibi Hayati

(? – 1853)

Bibi Hayati was born in the Kerman province of Persia (now Iraq) to a family with a long tradition of Sufi practice. She received her early training from her brother, who brought her to a Sufi gathering led by Nur 'Ali Shah, a master of the Nimatullahi Order. She became first his disciple, and later his wife. Hayati raised one child, a daughter, and also cooked and cared for members of the community at large until her death in 1853. Her poems offer us the Sufi realization that the radiance of the Beloved shines in and through all the many things of the world, making temple and alley equal when seen in their original Face.

Is this darkness the night of Power, or the black falling of your hair?
Is the rising light daybreak, or the reflection of your face?

In the book of Beauty, is this a first line?
Or merely a fragment I scribble, tracing your eyebrows?

Is this boxwood gathered in the orchard, or the rose garden's
    cypress?
The Tree of Paradise, heavy with dates, or the shape of your
    standing?

Is this scent from a Chinese deer, or the fragrance of infused water?
Is it the breathing of roses carried on wind, or your perfume?

Is this scorching a lightning bolt's remnants, or the burning
    mountain?
The heat of my sighs, or your inner body?

Is this Mongolian musk, or the purest of ambergris?
Is it the hyacinth unfolding, or your plaited curls?

Is this magic, or a chalice of red wine at dawn?
Your narcissus eye drunk with the way, or a sorcerer's work?

Is it the garden of Eden, or some earthly paradise?
The temple of those who have mastered the heart, or an alley?

Others all turn toward adobe and mud when they pray to the
    Sacred—
The temple of Hayati's soul turns toward the sun of your Face.

Before there was a trace of this world of men,
I carried the memory of a lock of your hair,
A stray end gathered within me, though unknown.

Inside that invisible realm,
Your face like the sun longed to be seen,
Until each separate object was finally flung into light.

From the moment of Time's first-drawn breath,
Love resides in us,
A treasure locked into the heart's hidden vault;

Before the first seed broke open the rose bed of Being,
An inner lark soared through your meadows,
Heading toward Home.

What can I do but thank you, one hundred times?
Your face illumines the shrine of Hayati's eyes,
Constantly present and lovely.

Emily Dickinson

(1830–1886)

Emily Dickinson was born December 10, 1830, into one of the prominent families of Amherst, Massachusetts. She was educated at Amherst Academy and attended Mount Holyoke Female Seminary for one year. During that time an evangelical religious revival was sweeping the country; when the principal asked "all those who wanted to be Christian" to rise from their seats, Emily was the only student who did not stand. In a letter sent in 1862 to Thomas Wentworth Higginson (poetry editor of The Atlantic *and Dickinson's sole literary confidant), she wrote, "I have a Brother and Sister—My Mother does not care for thought—and Father, too busy with his Briefs—to notice what we do—He buys me many Books—but begs me not to read them—because he fears they joggle the Mind. They [her family] are religious—except me—and address an Eclipse, every morning—whom they call their 'Father.'"*

Clearly, Dickinson's spirituality was not a conventional Christianity. Yet poem after poem, beginning in the early 1860s, shows the signs of some deep experience that shook her to the core, and led her to an understanding of "Heaven" as something available to us now as much as in any afterlife. Whether the precipitating event was, as many suspect, an erotic crisis, or some other kind of opening, or perhaps most likely a combination of both, the poems themselves stand as an unassailable testament to the experience's effect upon their author.

Following her return home from Mount Holyoke, Dickinson left Amherst only twice (once in 1855 and once, for treatment of an eye condition, in 1864), and for the last fifteen years of her life confined her activities solely to—as she called it—her father's house. In her later years, she dressed entirely in white. Yet in spite of this seemingly narrow existence, the 1,776 poems found after her death sewed neatly into pamphlets are models of freedom: freedom of thought, freedom of reference, freedom to take her own path of poetic technique, freedom of feeling. "My Business," she stated in another letter, "is Circumference"—and a vast world of imagination, observation, and precisely articulated spiritual and emotional experience is held within the circle of her words.

Who has not found the Heaven—below—
Will fail of it above—
For Angels rent the House next ours,
Wherever we remove—

(c. 1883)

I never saw a Moor—
I never saw the Sea—
Yet know I how the Heather looks
And what a Billow be.

I never spoke with God
Nor visited in Heaven—
Yet certain am I of the spot
As if the Checks were given—

(c. 1865)

Checks: chart

Death is a dialogue between
The spirit and the dust.
"Dissolve," says Death. The Spirit, "Sir,
I have another trust."

Death doubts it, argues from the ground.
The Spirit turns away,
Just laying off, for evidence,
An overcoat of clay.

(c. 1864)

The Props assist the House
Until the House is built
And then the Props withdraw
And adequate, erect,
The House support itself
And cease to recollect ·
The Auger and the Carpenter—
Just such a retrospect
Hath the perfected Life—
A past of Plank and Nail
And slowness—then the Scaffolds drop
Affirming it a Soul.

(c. 1863)

Dare you see a Soul *at the White Heat?*
Then crouch within the door—
Red—is the Fire's common tint—
But when the vivid Ore
Has vanquished Flame's conditions,
It quivers from the Forge
Without a color, but the light
Of unanointed Blaze.
Least Village has its Blacksmith
Whose Anvil's even ring
Stands symbol for the finer Forge
That soundless tugs—within—
Refining these impatient Ores
With Hammer, and with Blaze
Until the Designated Light
Repudiate the Forge—

(c. 1862)

I'm ceded—I've stopped being Theirs—
The name They dropped upon my face
With water, in the country church
Is finished using, now,
And They can put it with my Dolls,
My childhood, and the string of spools,
I've finished threading—too—

Baptized, before, without the choice,
But this time, consciously, of Grace—
Unto supremest name—
Called to my full—The Crescent dropped—
Existence's whole Arc, filled up,
With one small Diadem.

My second Rank—too small the first—
Crowned—Crowing—on my Father's breast—
A half unconscious Queen—
But this time—Adequate—Erect,
With Will to choose, or to reject,
And I choose—just a Crown—

(c. 1862)

'Tis little I—could care for Pearls—
Who own the ample sea—
Or brooches—when the Emperor—
With Rubies—pelteth me—

Or Gold—who am the Prince of Mines—
Or Diamonds—when have I
A Diadem to fit a Dome—
Continual upon me—

(c. 1862)

I had been hungry, all the Years—
My Noon had Come—to dine—
I trembling drew the Table near—
And touched the Curious Wine—

'Twas this on Tables I had seen—
When turning, hungry, Home
I looked in Windows, for the Wealth
I could not hope—for Mine—

I did not know the ample Bread—
'Twas so unlike the Crumb
The Birds and I, had often shared
In Nature's—Dining Room—

The Plenty hurt me—'twas so new—
Myself felt ill—and odd—
As Berry—of a Mountain Bush—
Transplanted—to the Road—

Nor was I hungry—so I found
That Hunger—was a way
Of Persons outside Windows—
The Entering—takes away—

(c. 1862)

Mine—by the Right of the White Election!
Mine—by the Royal Seal!
Mine—by the Sign in the Scarlet prison—
Bars—cannot conceal!

Mine—here—in Vision—and in Veto!
Mine—by the Grave's Repeal—
Titled—Confirmed—
Delirious Charter!
Mine—long as Ages steal!

(c. 1862)

Wild Nights—Wild Nights!
Were I with thee
Wild Nights should be
Our luxury!

Futile—the Winds—
To a Heart in port—
Done with the Compass—
Done with the Chart!

Rowing in Eden—
Ah, the Sea!
Might I but moor—Tonight—
In Thee!

(c. 1861)

The Infinite a sudden Guest
Has been assumed to be—
But how can that stupendous come
Which never went away?

(c. 1874)

Let me not thirst with this Hock at my Lip,
Nor beg, with Domains in my Pocket—

(c. 1881)

Hock: a kind of wine

A Georgia Sea Island Shout Song

(19th c.)

Although the importation of slaves was banned after 1807, the last illegal smuggling ship landed off the Georgia coast in 1858, and many of the songs collected there during the late nineteenth and early twentieth centuries show a particularly strong African influence. It is believed that the religious "shout" songs and their accompanying ring dance were derived from the North African Arabic saut (pronounced "shout"), the Islamic custom of circumambulating the Kaaba. Like all spirituals, these songs come from an anonymous oral tradition, but because we know of many secular traditional African songs that were obviously composed by women, and also that women serve as high priestesses in many African religions, it seems more than likely that women participated as well in the creation of this body of work.

The ring-shout given here was collected by Lydia Parrish, a Quaker who first heard the music of African-Americans in the 1870s in her New Jersey childhood Friends community (a long-time sanctuary for runaway slaves); later, after moving to St. Simon's Island in Georgia, she set out to preserve the old songs by instituting formal Sings at her home—though she reported that it was nine years before she was sufficiently trusted to see a shout performed. Describing "Down to the Mire," she wrote, "In the center of the ring, one member gets down on his knees, and, with head touching the floor, rotates with the group as it moves around the circle. The different shouters, as they pass, push the head 'down to the mire,' their several arms reaching out to give a push." She said of Josephine, whose words and singing she transcribed, that she would have a particularly far-off expression on her face as she sang, and that—though she was a woman heavy with both years and weight—she nonetheless bowed vigorously to the floor while performing this song about the unity of the low and the high, the heavenly and the earth.

Down to the Mire

Sister Emma, O you must come down to the mire
Sister Emma, O you must come down to the mire
    Jesus been down to the mire
    Jesus been down to the mire
    You must bow low to the mire
    Honor Jesus to the mire
    Honor Jesus to the mire
    Lower, lower to the mire
    Lower, lower to the mire
    Lower, lower to the mire
    Jesus been down to the mire

Sister Josie, you must come down to the mire
Sister Josie, you must come down to the mire
    Jesus been down to the mire
    Jesus been down to the mire
    Jesus been down to the mire
    Honor Jesus to the mire
    Honor Jesus to the mire
    Honor Jesus to the mire
    Honor Jesus to the mire
    Honor Jesus to the mire
    You must bow low to the mire
    You must bow low to the mire

(transcribed by Lydia Parrish; modernized by Al Young)

Penny Jessye's Deathbed Spiritual

(19th c.)

In 1927, Eva A. Jessye published My Spirituals, *in which she recorded the songs she had heard and sung while growing up in the small "Free Kansas" town of Coffeyville, populated mostly by former slaves from Georgia, Arkansas, Alabama and other parts of the South. The spiritual given here was sung by her ninety-year-old paternal grandmother, Penny Jessye, to whose deathbed Eva was called during her second year at college.*

Eva described their meeting this way: "On the morning I arrived, I found some eight or nine women sitting around her bed. There lay the wasted form of what had been a woman of gigantic stature. I had never seen my grandmother before and I stood gazing on the calm, set face which already bore an expression no longer human. The end was only a question of moments. Suddenly her eyes opened as if in response to a mysterious call. Their gaze roamed searchingly around the room until they rested on me. A smile of inexpressible joy lighted up her face as she murmured, 'So like, so like,' referring to my resemblance to my father. He was her favorite son and she had not seen him for many years. I knelt by the bedside and she spoke weakly. She stroked my bowed head, and in a faint whisper began singing a weird air, the words of which I could scarcely understand. The weight of her hand grew heavy and the voice quavered into silence . . . Her spirit ebbed its way to the Heaven her eyes of faith had long beheld.

"Most of grandmother's history is lost. It is, however, known that she was a full blooded South African and spent almost thirty years as a slave in Louisiana. After being freed she lived in Texas and Oswego, Kansas. She was noted for her majestic carriage, large physique, and great physical endurance . . . Many of the songs she sang were an odd mixture of crude English and African, utterly impossible to transcribe. But her hymn of farewell is clearly American in origin."

Good Lord
in That Heaven

Good Lord
In that Heaven,
Good Lord
In that Heaven,
Good Lord
In that Heaven,
I know I gotta home at last!

Go, Angel, and tell the news,
Go, Sister, and tell the news,
Go, Elder, and tell the news,
I know I gotta home at last!

(transcribed by Eva A. Jessye;
modernized by Al Young)

Christina Georgina Rossetti

(1830–1894)

Born in London, Christina Rossetti came from a family immersed in the arts. Her father was an Italian poet who, after fleeing Italy for political reasons, became a professor at King's College. Her brothers were the well-known pre-Raphaelite painter and poet Dante Gabriel Rossetti (Christina was the model for the Virgin in many of his paintings) and William Michael Rossetti, editor of an influential magazine; her older sister Maria wrote a study of Dante and later joined an Anglican order devoted to good works.

Christina, a prolific and inventive writer whose first collection was privately published when she was seventeen, left over 1,100 poems, a large portion of which are devotional in nature; her work was widely read and acclaimed during her lifetime. At the age of thirty, Rossetti fell deeply in love but refused to marry because her suitor did not share her religious views. Following an attack of Graves' disease at the age of forty-one, she became something of a recluse. Nonetheless, she continued to write until her death in 1894 from cancer, publishing poetry for both adults and children, as well as six volumes of devotional essays.

Rossetti's conception (in the second poem given here) of joy and pain as equal acts of praise is a theme that occurs in the work of many of the women in this book—how to understand the experience of suffering is one of the great ripening questions in virtually every spiritual tradition. A mature spirituality neither seeks out pain nor defends against it when it comes, and Rossetti's response is a mature one, of simple recognition and inclusion: "Ah, this too."

After Communion

Why should I call Thee Lord, Who art my God?
   Why should I call Thee Friend, Who art my Love?
   Or King, Who art my very Spouse above?
Or call Thy Sceptre on my heart Thy rod?
   Lo now Thy banner over me is love,
All heaven flies open to me at Thy nod:
For Thou hast lit Thy flame in me a clod,
   Made me a nest for dwelling of Thy Dove.
   What wilt Thou call me in our home above,
Who now has called me friend? how will it be
   When Thou for good wine settest forth the best?
Now Thou dost bid me come and sup with Thee,
   Now Thou dost make me lean upon Thy breast:
How will it be with me in time of love?

from Behold a Shaking

Blessed that flock safe penned in Paradise;
   Blessed this flock which tramps in weary ways;
   All form one flock, God's flock; all yield Him praise
By joy, or pain, still tending toward the prize.
Joy speaks in praises there, and sings and flies
   Where no night is, exulting all its days;
   Here, pain finds solace, for, behold, it prays;
In both love lives the life that never dies.
Here life is the beginning of our death,
   And death the starting-point whence life ensues;
    Surely our life is death, our death is life:
    Nor need we lay to hear our peace or strife,
But calm in faith and patience breathe the breath
   God gave, to take again when He shall choose.

Amen

It is over. What is over?
   Nay, how much is over truly:
Harvest days we toiled to sow for;
   Now the sheaves are gathered newly,
   Now the wheat is garnered duly.

It is finished. What is finished?
   Much is finished known or unknown:
Lives are finished; time diminished;
   Was the fallow field left unsown?
   Will these buds be always unblown?

It suffices. What suffices?
   All suffices reckoned rightly:
Spring shall bloom where now the ice is,
   Roses make the bramble sightly,
   And the quickening sun shine brightly,
   And the latter wind blow lightly,
And my garden teem with spices.

from Later Life: A Double Sonnet of Sonnets

Tread softly! all the earth is holy ground.
　　It may be, could we look with seeing eyes,
　　This spot we stand on is a Paradise
Where dead have come to life and lost been found,
Where Faith has triumphed, Martyrdom been crowned,
　　Where fools have foiled the wisdom of the wise;
　　From this same spot the dust of saints may rise,
And the King's prisoners come to light unbound.
O earth, earth, earth, hear thou thy Maker's Word:
　　"Thy dead thou shalt give up, nor hide thy slain" —
　　Some who went weeping forth shall come again
　　　　Rejoicing from the east or from the west,
As doves fly to their windows, love's own bird
　　　　Contented and desirous to the nest.

Uvavnuk

(19th c.)

Uvavnuk was an Iglulik Eskimo woman. The story of her transformation into a shaman is contained in Knud Rasmussen's Report of the Fifth Thule Expedition, 1921–1924, *Volume 7:*

> *Uvavnuk had gone outside the hut one winter evening to make water. It was particularly dark that evening, as the moon was not visible. Then suddenly there appeared a glowing ball of fire in the sky, and it came rushing down to earth straight towards her. She would have got up and fled, but before she could pull up her breeches, the ball of fire struck her and entered into her. At the same moment she perceived that all within her grew light, and she lost consciousness. But from that moment also she became a great shaman . . . The spirit of the meteor had entered into her and made her a shaman . . . She got up again, and without knowing what she was doing, came running into the house singing [the song below] . . . Shortly before her death she held a grand séance, and declared it was her wish that mankind should not suffer want, and she brought forth from the interior of the earth all manner of game which she had obtained . . . After her death, the people of her village had a year of greater abundance in whale, walrus, seal, and caribou than any had ever experienced before.* (translated from the Danish by W. Worster)

Among the Iglulik, women shamans were believed to be especially powerful.

The great sea
frees me, moves me,
as a strong river carries a weed.
Earth and her strong winds
move me, take me away,
and my soul is swept up in joy.

Two Kwakiutl Women's Prayers

(ca. 1895)

The following two women's prayers were collected in British Columbia by George Hunt for the anthropologist Franz Boas. The second prayer offers a somewhat startling formulation of the compact between human beings and the sacred abundance whose generosity sustains us through the gift of its body.

Prayer of a Woman in Charge of
Berry Picking in Knights Inlet

I come to you,
the one to whom I now pray,
the one whose means are mercy,
to ask that I may remain among the living.

Chief of the Upper World, Owner of Life,
may I come again next year
to stand again in this place
where I stand now to pray to you.

Prayer to the Sockeye Salmon

Welcome, o Supernatural One, o Swimmer,
who returns every year in this world
that we may live rightly, that we may be well.
I offer you, Swimmer, my heart's deep gratitude.

I ask that you will come again,
that next year we will meet in this life,
that you will see that nothing evil should befall me.
O Supernatural One, o Swimmer,
now I will do to you what you came here for me to do.

Owl Woman

(mid-19th–early 20th c.)

Owl Woman, whose Spanish name was Juana Maxwell, was a healer of the Papago tribe of the desert Southwest. During a time of extreme grief following the deaths of her husband and other relatives, Owl Woman was given her first medicine song by a spirit returned from the dead. She reported that it was the spirits who decided at that time that she should be a medicine woman, and so began teaching her songs. The ones following were collected by the remarkable anthropologist Frances Densmore during the 1920s.

The opening section of the healing ritual began at nightfall, and the first song depicts Owl Woman's spirit leaving her body at dusk during a shamanic trance. Densmore commented that the "rattling" sound of the darkness was a terrifying one for Owl Woman, and reported also that the "dawn" of the latter two poems is a reference to the light of the spirit world. She described Owl Woman as having "the appearance of a sybil, with a strange, far-seeing look in her eyes."

How shall I begin my song
In the blue night that is settling?

In the great night my heart will go out,
Toward me the darkness comes rattling.
In the great night my heart will go out.

Brown owls come here in the blue evening,
They are hooting about,
They are shaking their wings and hooting.

Black Butte is far.
Below it I had my dawn.
I could see the daylight
coming back for me.

The morning star is up.
I cross the mountains
into the light of the sea.

(all tr. by Frances Densmore)

An Osage Woman's Initiation Song

(early 20th c.)

This poem, collected by the Native American anthropologist Francis La Flesche, is sung at the end of the women's initiation rite in the Osage tribe, in which women were responsible for planting, cultivating, and harvesting corn. The poem is unusual in the way it places a mark of human identity at the sacred center of its world. Like many such songs and chants, it makes use of repetition as a way of calling forth order into the world.

Planting Initiation Song

I have made a footprint, a sacred one.
I have made a footprint, through it the blades push upward.
I have made a footprint, through it the blades radiate.
I have made a footprint, over it the blades float in the wind.
I have made a footprint, over it I bend the stalk to pluck the ears.
I have made a footprint, over it the blossoms lie gray.
I have made a footprint, smoke arises from my house.
I have made a footprint, there is cheer in my house.
I have made a footprint, I live in the light of day.

(*tr. by Francis La Flesche*)

A Traditional Navajo Prayer

(early 20th c.)

The Navajo Chantway ceremonies, among the most moving and lovely of all oral poetries, were sung mainly by men at the time of their recording by anthropologists, but were reported to have had their original source in Changing Woman, daughter of First Man and mother of the Navajo people. The selection below is from the female branch of the Shootingway ceremony, used to cure illnesses caused by lightning, snakes, or arrows. The nine-day-and-night-long sing from which it comes was performed by a medicine man named Red-Point for the benefit of his daughter Marie and recorded by Gladys A. Reichard, who had gone to the Navajo in the 1930s to study weaving. Recited in unison by Red-Point and his two daughters Marie and Ninaba, this prayer was repeated four times in front of a carefully selected young piñon tree as the final act of the ceremony.

Dark young pine, at the center of the earth originating,
I have made your sacrifice.
Whiteshell, turquoise, abalone beautiful,
Jet beautiful, fool's gold beautiful, blue pollen beautiful,
    reed pollen, pollen beautiful, your sacrifice I have made.
This day your child I have become, I say.

Watch over me.
Hold your hand before me in protection.
Stand guard for me, speak in defense of me.
As I speak for you, speak for me.
As you speak for me, so will I speak for you.
    May it be beautiful before me,
    May it be beautiful behind me,
    May it be beautiful below me,
    May it be beautiful above me,
    May it be beautiful all around me.

    I am restored in beauty.
    I am restored in beauty.
    I am restored in beauty.
    I am restored in beauty.

(tr. by Gladys A. Reichard)

H.D. (Hilda Doolittle)

(1886–1961)

H.D. (Hilda Doolittle) was raised in the Moravian town of Bethlehem, Pennsylvania. She attended Bryn Mawr briefly, during which time she met Marianne Moore, William Carlos Williams, and Ezra Pound. Both Williams and Pound became her close friends, and H.D. and Pound were briefly engaged, though it turned out that he had at the same time made a similar promise to another woman, whom he also did not marry. Pound nonetheless remained H.D.'s mentor and supporter; his encouragement that she study the poetry and cultures of the past became a determining factor in the nature of her later writing, which draws heavily upon ancient religious traditions and myths.

In 1911 H.D. left America for England, where she married the poet Richard Aldington and gave birth to a daughter, not his. The marriage ended in 1919, and H.D.'s lifelong companion after that was another woman, Bryher, who adopted H.D.'s daughter, Perdita, and with whom she eventually moved to Switzerland. Her books include poetry, translations, a novel, and a play.

As is true of much of the work in this book by women who lived through the wars, revolutions, and terrors of the twentieth century, H.D.'s later poetry is taken from the palette of a dark knowledge. In "The Walls Do Not Fall," her poem of the World War II London blitz, the task she set herself was finding a way to make of smoking ruined walls a temple open to the spiritual energies of past and present. H.D. (and Akhmatova, Mistral, Sachs, Södergran, Tsvetaeva, and Molodowsky) can be seen struggling to answer the question posed by Anna Akhmatova in her poem on page 208: "Why then do we not despair?" For each of them the answer is given in startlingly similar terms: in the broken-open heart there is a secret, a seed of inexplicable light that both nourishes and is fed.

White World

The whole white world is ours,
and the world, purple with rose-bays,
bays, bush on bush,
group, thicket, hedge and tree,
dark islands in a sea
of grey-green olive or wild white-olive,
cut with the sudden cypress shafts,
in clusters, two or three,
or with one slender, single cypress-tree.

Slid from the hill,
as crumbling snow-peaks slide,
citron on citron fill
the valley, and delight
waits till our spirits tire
of forest, grove and bush
and purple flower of the laurel-tree.

Yet not one wearies,
joined is each to each
in happiness complete
with bush and flower:
ours is the wind-breath
at the hot noon-hour,
ours is the bee's soft belly
and the blush of the rose-petal,
lifted, of the flower.

from The Walls Do Not Fall

[25]

Amen,
only just now,

my heart-shell
breaks open,

though long ago, the phoenix,
your *bennu* bird

dropped a grain,
as of scalding wax;

there was fragrance, burnt incense,
myrtle, aloes, cedar;

the Kingdom is a Tree
whose roots bind the heart-husk

to earth,
after the ultimate grain,

lodged in the heart-core,
has taken its nourishment.

from The Walls Do Not Fall

[36]

In no wise is the pillar-of-fire
that went before

different from the pillar-of-fire
that comes after;

chasm, schism in consciousness,
must be bridged over;

we are each, householder,
each with a treasure;

now is the time to re-value
our secret hoard

in the light of both past and future,
for whether

coins, gems, gold
beakers, platters,

or merely
talismans, records or parchments,

explicitly, we are told,
it contains

for every scribe
which is instructed,

things new
and old.

from Sagesse

[10]

Or is it a great tide that covers the rock-pool
so that it and the rock are indistinguishable

from the sea-shelf and are part of the sea-floor,
though the sea-anemone may quiver apprehensively

and the dried weed uncurl painfully
and the salt-sediment rebel, "I was salt,

a substance, concentrated, self-contained,
am I to be dissolved and lost?"

"it is fearful, I was a mirror, an individual,"
cries the shallow rock-pool, "now infinity

claims me; I am everything? but nothing";
peace, salt, you were never as useful as all that,

peace, flower, you are one of a thousand-thousand others,
peace, shallow pool, be lost.

Anna Akhmatova

(1889–1966)

Born in Odessa, Anna Akhmatova spent her youth in Tsarkoye Selo, the imperial retreat outside St. Petersburg. In 1910, she began an unhappy eight-year marriage with a well-known poet, Nikolai Gumilev, with whom she had one son. Along with Osip Mandelstam, they soon became leaders of the new Acmeist school of Russian poetry, marked by the use of language as a tool for precise meaning and by fidelity to the world of things and lived experience. As Akhmatova's work developed, this aesthetic grew into an increasingly strong sense of her mission in life: to bear witness as a poet to the experience of her compatriots, whatever it might be.

In 1921, Gumilev was executed by the Bolsheviks, and in 1925 Akhmatova, along with many of her poet contemporaries, was officially banned from publishing. She then earned her living by scholarship and translation, with only a brief respite during the 1940s when she was again permitted to publish. Throughout the harrowing decades of Stalinism, she suffered many of the sorrows of the Russian people—her son and her third husband were jailed, her husband eventually died while in confinement, and many of her closest friends were killed or committed suicide. Among the many poets who were casualties of the period were Mandelstam and Marina Tsvetaeva (see pages 231–236), also a friend of many years' standing. Known throughout this time for her personal integrity and courage, Akhmatova was finally rehabilitated after the dictator's death, and ended her life as an elder literary figure much beloved by both younger writers and the general public.

Everything is plundered, betrayed, sold,
Death's great black wing scrapes the air,
Misery gnaws to the bone.
Why then do we not despair?

By day, from the surrounding woods,
cherries blow summer into town;
at night the deep transparent skies
glitter with new galaxies.

And the miraculous comes so close
to the ruined, dirty houses—
something not known to anyone at all,
but wild in our breast for centuries.

(1921)

(tr. by Stanley Kunitz with Max Hayward)

A land not mine, still
forever memorable,
the waters of its ocean
chill and fresh.

Sand on the bottom whiter than chalk,
and the air drunk, like wine,
late sun lays bare
the rosy limbs of the pinetrees.

Sunset in the ethereal waves:
I cannot tell if the day
is ending, or the world, or if
the secret of secrets is inside me again.

(1964)

(tr. by Jane Kenyon)

Summer Garden

I want to visit the roses
In that lonely
Park where the statues remember me young
And I remember them under the water
Of the Neva. In that fragrant quiet
Between the limes of Tsarskoye I hear
A creak of masts. And the swan swims
Still, admiring its lovely
Double. And a hundred thousand steps,
Friend and enemy, enemy and friend,
Sleep. Endless is the procession of shades
Between granite vase and palace door.
There my white nights
Whisper of someone's discreet exalted
Love.
And everything is mother-
Of-pearl and jasper,
But the light's source is a secret.

(1959, July, Leningrad)

(tr. by D. M. Thomas)

Gabriela Mistral

(1889–1957)

Gabriela Mistral was born Lucila Godoy y Alcayaga in the Chilean village of Vicuna. Although Lucila was dismissed from school because she was thought "not gifted enough" to merit further instruction, she continued her studies on her own and eventually became a schoolteacher in a small town. There she fell passionately in love with a young railroad worker whose death by suicide in 1909 (because of a debt) changed the course of her life. Lucila's mourning took the form of an outpouring of poems, several of which won her a national poetry prize. It was at the time of their first publication in 1917 that she took her new name—Gabriela (after the archangel Gabriel) Mistral (after the famous wind of Provence).

Mistral's poetry and prose-poems became widely known throughout Latin America, and soon received international recognition, but she continued to teach, and eventually became famous as well in the field of educational reform, working particularly on programs for Indians and the rural poor. In 1920, a sixteen-year-old boy brought her his first verses. "You are a poet," she told him, "and you must keep writing. I have never said this to anyone before." The boy was Pablo Neruda.

Although Mistral had no children of her own, much of her work centers upon the theme of motherhood. In a "Poet's Note" to her first collection, Desolation, *she wrote that its poems (some of which had been criticized as crude and graphic in their descriptions of pregnancy) were "dedicated to those women capable of seeing that the sacredness of life begins with maternity which is, in itself, holy."* (tr. by Langston Hughes) *She did adopt a son, whom she called "Yin Yin"; his suicide at the age of seventeen mirrored the earlier tragedy in her life.*

When she was forty-two, Mistral traveled to the United States to teach Spanish history at several colleges. For the next twenty years she lived mostly abroad, serving her country as a "life consul" in various diplomatic posts, including Portugal, Brazil, and Italy. She became the first woman poet to receive the Nobel Prize for Literature, in 1945, and in 1953 she returned to the United States, where she lived until her death. Throughout her life she considered herself a voice for the powerless, especially women and children; her epitaph reads, "What the soul does for the body, the poet does for her people."

from Prayer

Like those jars that women put out to catch the dew of night,
I place my breasts before God. I give Him a new name, I call
Him the Filler, and I beg of Him the abundant liquid of life.
Thirstily looking for it, will come my son.

(tr. by Langston Hughes)

The Rose

The treasure at the heart of the rose
is your own heart's treasure.
Scatter it as the rose does:
your pain becomes hers to measure.

Scatter it in a song,
or in one great love's desire.
Do not resist the rose
lest you burn in its fire.

(tr. by Langston Hughes)

Those Who Do Not Dance

An invalid girl asked,
"How do I dance?"
We told her:
let your heart dance.

Then the crippled girl asked,
"How do I sing?"
We told her:
let your heart sing.

A poor dead thistle asked,
"How do I dance?"
We told it,
let your heart fly in the wind.

God asked from on high,
"How do I come down from this blueness?"
We told Him:
come dance with us in the light.

The entire valley is dancing
in a chorus under the sun.
The hearts of those absent
return to ashes.

(tr. by Maria Giachetti)

Song

A woman is singing in the valley. The shadows falling blot her out, but her song spreads over the fields.

Her heart is broken, like the jar she dropped this afternoon among the pebbles in the brook. As she sings, the hidden wound sharpens on the thread of her song, and becomes thin and hard. Her voice in modulation dampens with blood.

In the fields the other voices die with the dying day, and a moment ago the song of the last slow-poke bird stopped. But her deathless heart, alive with grief, gathers all the silent voices into her voice, sharp now, yet very sweet.

Does she sing for a husband who looks at her silently in the dusk, or for a child whom her song caresses? Or does she sing for her own heart, more helpless than a babe at nightfall?

Night grows maternal before this song that goes to meet it; the stars, with a sweetness that is human, are beginning to come out; the sky full of stars becomes human and understands the sorrows of this world.

Her song, as pure as water filled with light, cleanses the plain and rinses the mean air of day in which men hate. From the throat of the woman who keeps on singing, day rises nobly evaporating toward the stars.

(tr. by Langston Hughes)

Nelly Sachs

(1891–1970)

Born to an assimilated family in Berlin, Nelly Sachs first began to explore her Jewish heritage in 1933, after the advent of Nazism brought her to a heightened awareness of her background. In 1940, on the verge of being deported to a concentration camp, she and a few others (though not the man she was in love with, who died in the camps) escaped to Stockholm with the help of a novelist who, though they knew each other only through correspondence, interceded on Sachs's behalf with the Swedish royal family. Once there, she moved into a one-room apartment with her mother, learned Swedish, and began working as a translator of German poetry. For the rest of her life, the Holocaust remained the theme underlying all her writing.

In 1966, Sachs shared the Nobel Prize in Literature with the Israeli novelist S. I. Agnon; the prize citation commended Sachs for her "works of forgiveness, of deliverance, of peace." Her poems find their spiritual authority and consolation in Sachs's refusal to close her eyes or her ears to the ways of a God who lives even in terror and suffering, even in absence and death. Their power comes from the poet's absolutely unmixed attention—Simone Weil's definition of prayer.

How long have we forgotten how to listen!

"Before they spring forth I tell you of them"
                                                —Isaiah 42:9

How long have we forgotten how to listen!
He planted us once to listen
Planted us like lyme grass by the eternal sea,
We wanted to grow on fat pastures,
To stand like lettuce in the kitchen garden.

Although we have business
That leads us far
From his light,
Although we drink tap water,
And only as it dies it reaches
Our eternally thirsting mouths—
Although we walk down a street
Beneath which earth has been silenced
By a pavement,
We must not sell our ears,
Oh, we must not sell our ears.
Even in the market,
In the computation of dust,
Many had made a quick leap
Onto the tightrope of longing.
Because they heard something,
And leapt out of the dust
And sated their ears.
Press, oh press in the day of destruction
The listening ear to the earth,
And you will hear, through your sleep

You will hear,
How in death
Life begins.

*(tr. by Ruth and
Matthew Mead)*

Your eyes, O my beloved

"I saw that he saw"
        —Jehuda Zwi

Your eyes, O my beloved
Were the eyes of a hind,
With pupils of long rainbows
As when storms of God are gone—
Bee-like the centuries stored there
The honey of God's nights,
Last sparks of Sinai's fires—
O you transparent doors
To the inner realms,
Over which so much desert sand lies,
So many miles of torment to reach O Him—
O you lifeless eyes
Whose power of prophecy has fallen
Into the golden astonishments of the Lord,
Of which we know only the dreams.

(tr. by Ruth and Matthew Mead)

Someone

Someone
will take the ball
from the hands that play
the game of terror.

Stars
have their own law of fire
and their fertility
is the light
and reapers and harvesters
are not native here.

Far off
stand their granaries
straw too
has a momentary power of illumination
painting loneliness.

Someone will come
and sew the green of the spring bud
on their prayer shawl
and set the child's silken curl
as a sign
on the brow of the century.

Here Amen
must be said
this crowning of words
which moves into hiding
and
peace
you great eyelid

closing on all unrest
your heavenly wreath of lashes

You most gentle of all births.

(tr. by Ruth and Matthew Mead)

Rushing at times like flames

Rushing at times
like flames through our bodies—
as if they were still woven with the beginning
of the stars.

How slowly we flash up in clarity—

Oh, after how many lightyears have our hands
folded in supplication—
our knees bent—
and our souls opened
in thanks?

(tr. by Ruth and Matthew Mead)

In the evening your vision widens

In the evening your vision widens
looks out beyond midnight—
twofold I stand before you—
green bud rising out of dried-up sepal,
in the room where we are of two worlds.
You too already extend far beyond the dead,
those who are here,
and know of what has flowered
out of the earth with its bark of enigma.

As in the womb the unborn
with the primordial light on its brow
has the rimless view
from star to star—
So ending flows to beginning
like the cry of a swan.
We are in a sickroom.
But the night belongs to the angels.

(tr. by Michael Roloff)

But perhaps God needs the longing

But perhaps God needs the longing, wherever else should it dwell,
Which with kisses and tears and sighs fills mysterious spaces of air—
And perhaps is invisible soil from which roots of stars grow and
    swell—
And the radiant voice across fields of parting which calls to reunion
    there?
O my beloved, perhaps in the sky of longing worlds have been born
    of our love—
Just as our breathing, in and out, builds a cradle for life and death?
We are grains of sand, dark with farewell, lost in births' secret
    treasure trove,
Around us already perhaps future moons, suns, and stars blaze in a
    fiery wreath.

(tr. by Ruth and Matthew Mead)

Edith Södergran

(1892–1923)

In 1892, when Edith Södergran was born, Finland was a part of Imperial Russia. Throughout her childhood, her family—members of the Swedish-speaking minority of the Finnish population—moved back and forth between St. Petersburg and their country home fifty kilometers to the north in the village of Raivola. Educated in German, French, and Russian, Södergran spoke Swedish only at home, and her first poems were written in German.

In 1907 Södergran's father died of tuberculosis, and two years later Edith was also diagnosed as having the disease. She spent the next few years in various sanitoria; it was during this time that she determined to write in her native tongue. Upon her return to Raivola, she fell deeply in love with a married man, but the affair ended badly. Södergran's later poems about the relationship between the sexes, and about friendship between women, bear a strong feminist slant. With the Russian Revolution, civil war came to Finland as well, and amid the disorder and strife Södergran came close to starvation. The family survived by selling their furniture and household goods, even underclothing and bottles of perfume.

Södergran began publishing her poetry in 1916. Written without rhyme or meter, it was poorly received by a literary community not yet familiar with modernism, and although she has since come to be considered a major figure in Scandinavian letters, her work was never widely recognized during her lifetime. Nonetheless, she did not waver in her belief in its importance: in the preface to one book she wrote, "My self-confidence depends on the fact that I have discovered my dimensions. It does not become me to make myself less than I am."

In addition to poetry, Södergran occasionally wrote series of aphorisms. Two of them help illuminate her conception of the spiritual, which was influenced by her study of the works of Goethe and Rudolf Steiner: "Nature's path to God is direct, eternal, and objective, without external chance." And, "The human heart that seeks God has to struggle against subjectivity, for the heart begins on the other side of subjectivity. But the path of nature is protected." As she neared her death (of tuberculosis, at the age of thirty-one), this intensely subjective poet wrote, "certainty comes to you, and the answer to every riddle./And you shall praise God who lets you stand in his temple/among the trees and the stones." (translations by David McDuff)

On Foot I Had to Walk Through
the Solar Systems

On foot
I had to walk through the solar systems,
before I found the first thread of my red dress.
Already, I sense myself.
Somewhere in space hangs my heart,
sparks fly from it, shaking the air,
to other reckless hearts.

(tr. by Stina Katchadourian)

"There is no one . . ."

There is no one in this world who has time
but God alone.
And therefore all flowers come to Him
and the least among the ants.

The forget-me-not asks Him for a stronger brilliance
in her blue eyes
and the ant asks Him for more strength
to grip the straw.
And the bees ask Him for a stronger victory song
among scarlet roses.

And God is present in everything.
When the old woman unexpectedly met her cat at the well
and the cat his mistress
the joy was great for both of them
but greater still was their knowledge that God had brought them
      together
and wished them this wonderful friendship
for fourteen years.

Meanwhile, a redstart flew out of the mountain ash by the well
happy that God had not allowed the hunter to catch him.
But in a vague dream a little worm saw
how the crescent moon split his being into two:
one was nothing,
the other one was everything and God Himself.

(tr. by Stina Katchadourian)

Forest Lake

I was alone on a sunny shore
by the forest's pale blue lake,
in the sky floated a single cloud
and on the water a single isle.
The ripe sweetness of summer dripped
in beads from every tree
and straight into my opened heart
a tiny drop ran down.

(tr. by Stina Katchadourian)

Question

I need nothing but God's mercy.
I go through life in a drunken stupor.

O you strangely lightening reality—
-------- is there an amphora
for my few drops of oil of roses?

(tr. by David McDuff)

Homecoming

My childhood's trees stand rejoicing around me: O human!
and the grass bids me welcome from foreign lands.
I lean my head in the grass: now home at last.
Now I shall turn my back on all that lies behind me:
my only comrades shall be the forest and the shore and the lake.

Now I shall drink wisdom from the spruces' sap-filled crowns,
now I shall drink truth from the withered trunks of the birches,
now I shall drink power from the smallest and tenderest grasses:
a mighty protector mercifully reaches me his hand.

(tr. by David McDuff)

Marina Tsvetaeva

(1892–1941)

Marina Tsvetaeva was born in Moscow, the daughter of an art historian father and a pianist mother who died when Tsvetaeva was fourteen. Marina published her first book of poetry at the age of sixteen, and was immediately made welcome in the circle of Symbolist poets. In 1912, she married a fellow aspiring writer, Sergey Efron, with whom she had two children. During the first World War Efron served with the Russian Army and after the Revolution, with the White Guard. Meanwhile Tsvetaeva took odd jobs in bakeries and libraries, occasionally resorting to theft in the attempt to keep her children alive, although the younger one died of malnutrition in 1920.

After five years during which she did not know her husband's fate, Tsvetaeva joined him in 1922 in a life of exile and poverty, first in Prague, then in Paris. Although they lived among other emigré White Russians, Sergey came to be suspected (correctly) of being a Soviet informer and assassin—an aspect of his life of which Tsvetaeva was entirely ignorant. They had one other child, a son. In 1939 Tsvetaeva followed her husband back to the Soviet Union, where Sergey was soon arrested and executed by the secret police despite his previous collaboration. Penniless, with little opportunity for paying work and none for publishing, and ostracized by most members of the literary community, Tsvetaeva hanged herself in August 1941.

I know the truth

I know the truth—give up all other truths!
No need for people anywhere on earth to struggle.
Look—it is evening, look, it is nearly night:
what do you speak of, poets, lovers, generals?

The wind is level now, the earth is wet with dew,
the storm of stars in the sky will turn to quiet.
And soon all of us will sleep under the earth, we
who never let each other sleep above it.

(1915)

(tr. by Elaine Feinstein)

I bless the daily labor

I bless the daily labor of my hands,
I bless the sleep that nightly is my own.
The mercy of the Lord, the Lord's commands,
The law of blessings and the law of stone.

My dusty purple, with its ragged seams . . .
My dusty staff, where all light's rays are shed.
And also, Lord, I bless the peace
In others' houses—others' ovens' bread.

(21 May 1918)

(tr. by David McDuff)

If the soul was born with pinions

If the soul was born with pinions
What are hovels to it, what are mansions?
What's Genghis Khan to it and what his Horde?
I have two enemies in all the world,
Two twins, inseparably fused:
The hunger of the hungry and the fullness of the full.

(18 August 1918)

(tr. by David McDuff)

God (3)

No, you never will bind him
To your signs and your burdens!
The least chink—he's inside it,
Like the supplest of gymnasts.

By the drawbridges
And flocks in migration,
By the telegraph poles,
God's escaping us.

No, you never will train him
To abide and to share!
He, in feelings' resident slush,
Is a gray floe of ice.

No, you never will catch him!
On a thrifty dish, God
Never thrives in the window
Like domestic begonias!

All, beneath the roof's vault,
Were awaiting the builder,
The call. Poets and pilots
—All gave up in despair.

He's the sprint—and he's moving.
The whole volume of stars
Is, from Alpha to Omega,
Just a trace of his cloak.

(1922)

(tr. by Paul Graves)

The gold that was my hair has turned
silently to gray. Don't pity me!
Everything's been realized,
in my breast all's blended and attuned.

—Attuned, as all of distance blends
In the smokestack moaning on the outskirts.
And Lord! A soul's been realized:
The most deeply secret of your ends.

(1922)

(tr. by Paul Graves)

Kadya Molodowsky

(1894–1975)

Among Ashkenazic Jews, there is a type of prose prayer for women known as tkhines, composed in Yiddish rather than the liturgical Hebrew. The recitation of these prayers might accompany such ceremonial household tasks as the making of holiday candles or the baking of the Sabbath bread, or it might serve as part of the celebration of the Sabbath itself. Such a prayer might also be offered as the more spontaneous speech of a heart seeking guidance and comfort.

The influence of these prayers that make holy the things and tasks of everyday life is found in the work of many of the Yiddish women poets who flourished early in the twentieth century, and can be seen here in one of a series of prayer-poems written by Kadya Molodowsky. Reading it with care, we see that the poet is not asking to escape the sorrows and fears of her everyday life, but to be permitted to know that life fully, even while suffering—asking to be not an unfeeling stone cast on hard ground, but a field in which what is fathomless can grow. In simplicity, her poem tells us, the sacred enters us and we enter the sacred. It is as simple as the everyday occurrence of a seed of grass taking root in the earth, and the earth, in turn, becoming the grass which rises: part of its living body.

Born in Lithuania in 1894, Molodowsky began publishing poetry in her twenties. She moved to Warsaw with her husband, where she taught in Yiddish schools and practiced journalism. In 1935, she moved to New York, where she co-founded and edited a Yiddish literary journal. She published six books of poems over her life as well as fiction, plays, and essays, and traveled extensively in Israel, where she was awarded a major literary prize in 1971. She died in 1975.

Prayers: I

Don't let me fall
As a stone falls upon the hard ground.
And don't let my hands become dry
As the twigs of a tree
When the wind beats down the last leaves.
And when the storm raises dust from the earth
With anger and howling,
Don't let me become the last fly
Trembling terrified on a windowpane.
Don't let me fall.
I have asked for so much,
But as a blade of your grass in a distant wild field
Lets drop a seed in the lap of the earth
And dies away,
Sow in me your living breath,
As you sow a seed in the earth.

(tr. by Kathryn Hellerstein)

Sub-ok

(1902–1966)

Sub-ok was born in the southern coastal town of Chinhae, near Pusan, Korea, in 1902. At sixteen, the usual age for marriage, she left home secretly; turned down by the first temple where she sought ordination because it did not accept women, she eventually made her way to Sudok-sa Temple, where she became a Buddhist nun. After studying with a number of respected teachers of Zen in both Korea and Japan, she taught in various monks' colleges and in 1955 was made the head of a temple of her own, whose rebuilding she supervised after its destruction during the Korean War. She died there in 1966 at the age of sixty-four. The spring breeze of her poem—continuing its serenely wholehearted practice at the crossroad of what stays and what departs—seems an appropriate image with which to end this book.

Spring at Yesan Station

The steam whistle cleaves to the wind
    As the train speeds over one thousand mountains.
White clouds hang leisurely in the sky
    Over the station bidding farewell.
The spring breeze spins a humming song
    In the branches of a green willow at the crossroads,
Waving its cane as it returns, chanting alone.

(tr. by Julie Pickering)

A Note on the Translations

All English versions not otherwise identified were made by Jane Hirshfield, either from the original or, if from other translations, from multiple scholarly sources wherever possible. Sources for all such versions appear in the following "For Further Reading" section.

For Further Reading

For a scholarly survey of religious writings related to women worldwide, see *An Anthology of Sacred Texts by and About Women*, edited by Serinity Young (New York: Crossroad, 1993). Also, a number of indispensable comprehensive anthologies of women's poetry were compiled and published in the 1970s and 1980s; all contain work by some of the women found in this collection, and all were extremely helpful in the preliminary research for this book.

Page

3. For a full, scholarly translation of Enheduanna's poem and more information about Enheduanna and her times, see *The Exaltation of Inanna*, by William W. Hallo and J. J. A. Van Dijk (New Haven and London: Yale University Press, 1968). Other material about the moon-goddess Inanna, though not necessarily from the work of women writers, is assembled in *Inanna, Queen of Heaven and Earth*, by Diane Wolkstein and Samuel Noah Kramer (New York: Harper & Row, 1983).

8. Shu-Sin's Ritual Bride's poem and a description of the Inanna-Dumuzi material and of Sumerian poetry in general can be found in *The Sacred Marriage Rite: Aspects of Faith, Myth, and Ritual in Ancient Sumer*, by Samuel Noah Kramer (Bloomington and London: Indiana University Press, 1969). Another version of the poem appears in *The Harps That Once . . . : Sumerian Poetry in Translation* by Thorkild Jacobsen (New Haven and London: Yale University Press, 1987).

11. These words of Queen Makeda have come down to us in the *Kebra Nagast*, the "Glory of the Kings [of Ethiopia]." For a full prose translation, see *The Queen of Sheba and her only Son Menyelek*, translated by Sir E. A. Wallis Budge (London, Liverpool, and Boston: The Medici Society, Limited, 1922). I am grateful to *Daughters of Africa, An International Anthology of Words and Writings by Women of African Descent from the Ancient Egyptian to the Present*, edited by Margaret Busby (New York: Pantheon, 1992), which drew this material to my attention.

15. There have been many translations of Sappho's poetry. Among the most admired is *Sappho: A New Translation*, by Mary Barnard (Berkeley: University of California Press, 1958). Diane Rayor's translation is from *Sappho's Lyre: Archaic Lyric & Women Poets of Ancient Greece* (Berkeley: University of California

Press, 1991); also see *Sappho: A Garland* by Jim Powell (New York: Farrar, Straus and Giroux, 1993).

18. For more on Sumangalamata, Patacara, and the other early Pali women poets, see *The First Buddhist Women: Translations and Commentary on the Therigatha*, by Susan Murcott (Berkeley: Parallax Press, 1991). Poems from the *Therigatha* also appear in a number of earlier collections, many published by the Pali Text Society, and in several anthologies of women's poetry.

21. The Zi Ye poem translated here is from *Translations from the Chinese*, by Arthur Waley (New York: Alfred A. Knopf, 1919). Others appear in *The Lotus Lovers*, translated by Sam Hamill (Saint Paul: Coffee House Press, 1985) and in most large anthologies of Chinese poetry.

22. Many translations of "The Song of Songs" exist; the excerpts here are from *The Song of Songs*, translated by Ariel and Chana Bloch (New York: Random House, 1994).

29. For full scholarly versions of "The Thunder: Perfect Mind" see *The Nag Hammadi Library in English*, James M. Robinson, general editor (San Francisco: Harper & Row, 1988) and *The Gnostic Scriptures*, translated and edited by Bentley Layton (New York: Doubleday & Co., 1987). See also *The Gnostic Gospels*, by Elaine Pagels (New York: Random House, 1979), for a discussion of this material and its background.

34. For other examples of Graeco-Roman women's religious texts, see *Maenads, Martyrs, Matrons, Monastics*, edited by Ross S. Kraemer (Philadelphia: Fortress Press, 1988).

36. Sabina Lampadius's poem is from *Cybele and Attis: The Myth and the Cult*, by Maarten J. Vermaseren; translated from the Dutch by A. M. H. Lemmers (London: Thames and Hudson, 1977). Other inscriptions appear in *Maenads, Martyrs, Matrons, Monastics*; see previous entry.

39. For more on Antal, see *Antal and Her Path of Love*, by Vidya Dehajai (Albany: SUNY Press, 1990). Many other English translations of her work have been published in India and are available in larger university libraries.

42. For more on Rabi'a, see *Rabi'a the Mystic and Her Fellow Saints in Islam*, by Margaret Smith (Cambridge: Cambridge University Press, 1928); *Doorkeeper of the Heart: Versions of Rabi'a*, translated by Charles Upton (Putney, VT: Threshold Books, 1988); *Sufi Women*, by Dr. Javad Nurbakhsh, translated by Leonard Lewisohn (New York: Khaniqahi-Nimatullahi Publications, 1983); and *Women Saints East and West*, editorial advisor Swami Ghanananda (Hollywood: Vedanta Press, 1979).

46. For more on Yeshe Tsogyel see *Sky Dancer: The Secret Life and Songs of the Lady Yeshe Tsogyel*, by Keith Dowman (London: Routledge & Kegan Paul, 1984); *The Lotus-Born: The Life of Padmasambhava, by the Lady Yeshe Tsogyel*, edited by Marcia Binder Schmidt and translated by Erik Pema Kunsang (Boston:

Shambhala Publications, 1993); and *Feminine Ground: Essays on Women and Tibet*, edited by Janice D. Willis (Ithaca, NY: Snow Lion Publications, 1989).

48. For more on Lakshminkara see Miranda Shaw's essay in *Feminine Ground: Essays on Women and Tibet*, edited by Janice D. Willis (Ithaca, NY: Snow Lion Publications, 1989).

51. For a discussion of the work and lives of Indian women Tantric practitioners see *Passionate Enlightenment: Women and Tantric Buddhism in India*, by Miranda Shaw (Princeton: Princeton University Press, 1994).

53. For more on Kassiane, see "Kassiane the Nun and the Sinful Woman," by Eva Catafygiotu Topping, in *The Greek Orthodox Theological Review*, Volume 26, Fall 1981, pp. 201–209.

55. For more of Yu Xuanji's poems, see *A Book of Women Poets from Antiquity to Now*, edited by Aliki Barnstone and Willis Barnstone (New York: Schocken Books: 1980); *Sunflower Splendor: Three Thousand Years of Chinese Poetry*, edited by Wu-chi Liu and Irving Yucheng Lo (Garden City, NY: Anchor Books, 1975); and *The Orchid Boat: Women Poets of China*, translated and edited by Kenneth Rexroth and Ling Chung (New York: The Seabury Press, 1972).

57. For more about Izumi Shikibu and her poems, see *The Ink Dark Moon: Love Poems by Ono no Komachi and Izumi Shikibu*, translated by Jane Hirshfield with Mariko Aratani (New York: Vintage Classics, 1990).

64. For more of Li Qingzhao's poetry, see *Li Ch'ing-chao: Complete Poems*, translated and edited by Kenneth Rexroth and Ling Chung, New Directions, NY 1979; *As Though Dreaming: The Tz'u of Pure Jade*, by Li Ch'ing-chao, translated by Lenore Mayhew and William McNaughton (Tokyo: Mushinsha Ltd., 1977); and *The Lotus Lovers*, translated by Sam Hamill (Saint Paul: Coffee House Press, 1985).

66. For all of Hildegard of Bingen's poetry, including the original Latin and literal translations, see *Symphonia: A Critical Edition of the Symphonia armonie celestium revelationum*, with introduction, translations, and commentary by Barbara Newman (Ithaca and London: Cornell University Press, 1988); for a study of her thought, see *Sister of Wisdom: St. Hildegard's Theology of the Feminine*, by Barbara Newman (Berkeley: University of California Press, 1987). See also a recent prose translation of the *Scivias*, translated by Mother Columba Hart and Jane Bishop (Rahway, NJ: Paulist Press, 1990) and *Hildegard of Bingen's Book of Divine Works, with Letters and Songs*, edited by Matthew Fox (Santa Fe: Bear & Co., 1987). A good, brief biography appears in *Women Mystics in Medieval Europe*, by Emilie Zum Brunn and Georgette Epiney-Burgard, translated from the French by Sheila Hughes (New York: Paragon House, 1989).

73. For more of Sun Bu-er's writing, both poetry and prose, see *Immortal Sisters:*

Secrets of Taoist Women, translated and edited by Thomas Cleary (Boston: Shambhala Publications, 1989).

75. For more of Zhou Xuanjing's poetry, see *Immortal Sisters: Secrets of Taoist Women*, edited and translated by Thomas Cleary (Boston: Shambhala Publications, 1989).

76. For more of Cui Shaoxuan's poetry, see *Immortal Sisters: Secrets of Taoist Women*, edited and translated by Thomas Cleary (Boston: Shambhala Publications, 1989).

77. For more work by Mahadeviyakka, see *Women Saints East and West*, editorial advisor Swami Ghanananda (Hollywood: Vedanta Press, 1979); *Women Writing in India* edited by Susie Tharu and K. Lalita (New York: The Feminist Press, 1991); *A Book of Women Poets from Antiquity to Now*, edited by Aliki Barnstone and Willis Barnstone (New York: Schocken Books, 1980); *Speaking of Siva*, edited by A. K. Ramanujan (Penguin Classics, London and New York, 1973); *Some Kannada Poems*, translated by A. K. Ramanujan and M. G. Krishnamurthi (Calcutta: Writers Workshop, Lake Garden Press, 1967); and *Mahadevi*, by Dr. Siddhayya Puranik, translated by G. B. Sajjan (Dharwad, India: The Insitute of Kannada Studies, Karnatak University, 1986).

85. For more on Mechtild of Magdeburg, see *Women Saints East and West*, editorial advisor Swami Ghanananda (Hollywood: Vedanta Press, 1979); *The Revelations of Mechtild of Magdeburg*, by Lucy Menzies (New York: Longmans, Green, 1953); *Beguine Spirituality: Mystical Writings of Mechtild of Magdeburg, Beatrice of Nazareth, and Hadewijch of Brabant*, edited and introduced by Fiona Bowie, translated by Oliver Davies (New York: Crossroad Publishing Company, 1989); and *Jesus as Mother: Studies in the Spirituality of the High Middle Ages*, by Caroline Walker Bynum (Berkeley and Los Angeles: University of California Press, 1982). *Women Mystics of Medieval Europe*, by Emilie Zum Brunn and Georgette Epiney-Burgard, translated from the French by Sheila Hughes (New York: Paragon House, 1989) and *Medieval Women's Visionary Literature*, by Elizabeth Alvilda Petroff (New York/Oxford: Oxford University Press, 1986) also contain good accounts of Mechtild's life and work.

97. For more about Marguerite Porete, see *Women Writers of the Middle Ages: A Critical Study of Texts from Perpetua (d. 203) to Margeurite Porete (d. 1310)*, by Peter Dronke (Cambridge: Cambridge University Press, 1984); *Women Mystics of Medieval Europe* by Emilie Zum Brunn and Georgette Epiney-Burgard, translated from the French by Sheila Hughes (New York: Paragon House, 1989); and *Medieval Women's Visionary Literature*, by Elizabeth Alvilda Petroff (New York/Oxford: Oxford University Press, 1986).

99. For more about Hadewijch, see *Hadewijch: The Complete Works*, translated and introduced by Mother Columba Hart, O.S.B. (Mahwah, New Jersey: The Paulist Press, 1980); *Passionate Women: Two Medieval Mystics* by Eliza-

beth Dreyer (Mahwah, NJ: The Paulist Press, 1989); and *Beguine Spirituality: Mystical Writings of Mechtild of Magdeburg, Beatrice of Nazareth, and Hadewijch of Brabant*, edited and introduced by Fiona Bowie, translated by Oliver Davies (New York: Crossroad Publishing Company, 1989). *Women Mystics of Medieval Europe* and *Medieval Women's Visionary Literature* (see previous entry) also contain information on Hadewijch.

105. For a discussion of the question of Hadewijch II and Hadewijch I, see *The Measure of Mystic Thought: A Study of Hadewijch's Mengeldichten* by S. M. Murk Jansen (Stuttgart: Kummerle Verlag, Goppingen, 1991).

114. For more work by Janabai, see *Women Writing in India*, edited by Susie Tharu and K. Lalita (New York: The Feminist Press, 1991) and *A Book of Women Poets from Antiquity to Now*, edited by Aliki Barnstone and Willis Barnstone (New York: Schocken Books, 1980).

116. For full translations of twenty-six of Catherine's ecstatic prayers, see *The Prayers of Catherine of Siena*, edited and translated by Suzanne Noffke, O.P. (Ramsey, NJ: Paulist Press, 1983). For a contemporary biographical account, see *The Life of Catherine of Siena* by Raymond of Capua, translated by Conleth Kearns, O.P. (Wilmington: Michael Glazier, 1980).

118. For more about Lal Děd, see *Women Saints East and West*, edited by Swami Ghanananda and Sir John Stewart-Wallace, C.B. (Hollywood, CA: Vedanta Press, 1979). Coleman Barks's translations can be found in *Lalla: Naked Song*, © 1992, available from Maypop Books, 196 Westview Drive, Athens, Georgia 30606; Willis Barnstone's translation is from *A Book of Women Poets from Antiquity to Now*, edited by Aliki and Willis Barnstone (New York: Schocken Books, 1980). See also *Lalla-Vakyani, or The Wise Sayings of Lal Ded, A Mystic Poetess of Ancient Kashmir*, edited by Sir George Grierson and Lionel D. Barnett (London: The Royal Asiatic Society, 1920).

128. For more on Vittoria Colonna, see "Vittoria Colonna: Child, Woman, and Poet," in *Women Writers of the Renaissance and Reformation*, edited by Katharina M. Wilson (Athens and London: University of Georgia Press, 1987). Colonna's poetry also appears in a manuscript in progress, *Courtly Ladies and Courtesans of the Italian Renaissance*, edited and translated by Laura Anna Stortoni and Mary Prentice Lillie.

131. For further reading on Mirabai, see *Mirabai Versions*, by Robert Bly (Red Ozier Press, 1980; expanded version Penland, NC: Squid, Ink, 1993); *The Devotional Poems of Mirabai*, translated by A. J. Alston (Motilal Banarsidass, India, 1980); *For Love of the Dark One*, translated by Andrew Schelling (Boston: Shambhala Publications, 1993); *Mira Bai* by Usha S. Nilsson (New Delhi: Sahitya Akademi, 1969); *Bhakta Mira* by Bankey Behari (Chaupatty, Bombay: Bharatiya Vidya Bhavan, 1971); *The Story of Mira Bai*, by Bankey Behari (Gorakhpur: Gita Press, 1935).

143. There are many books about the life of Teresa of Avila as well as those that col-

lect her writings. A full translation of her writings can be found in *The Complete Works of St. Teresa*, translated and edited by E. Allison Peers, three volumes (London: Sheed and Ward, 1946). The quotes in the biographical information given here come from *Mother of Carmel* by E. Allison Peers (New York: Morehouse-Gorham Co., 1946).

145. This poem by Maria de' Medici comes from a manuscript in progress, *Courtly Ladies and Courtesans of the Italian Renaissance*, edited and translated by Laura Anna Stortoni and Mary Prentice Lillie.

146. More translations from the Nahuatl can be found in *Snake Poems: An Aztec Invocation* by Francisco X. Alarcón (San Francisco: Chronicle Books, 1992). That collection also includes a full bibliography of works related to Hernando Ruiz de Alarcón and ancient Mexican poetry in general. One of several full editions of the "Treatise" is *Aztec Sorcerers in Seventeenth Century Mexico: The Treatise on Superstitions by Hernando Ruiz de Alarcón*, translated and edited by Michael D. Coe and Gordon Whittaker (Albany, NY: Institute for Mesoamerican Studies, SUNY, 1982).

149. For the complete works of Anne Bradstreet, see *The Works of Anne Bradstreet*, edited by Jeannine Hensley (Cambridge: The Belknap Press of Harvard University Press, 1967). For an excellent reevaluation of Puritan poetry and its themes, see *God's Altar: The World and the Flesh in Puritan Poetry*, by Robert Daly (Berkeley: University of California Press, 1978).

155. For a full discussion of the life of Sor Juana de la Cruz see *Sor Juana, or, The Traps of Faith* by Octavio Paz, translated by Margaret Sayers Peden (Cambridge: The Belknap Press of Harvard University Press, 1988). For more of her poetry, see *A Sor Juana Anthology*, translated by Alan S. Trueblood (Cambridge: Harvard University Press, 1988) and *Sor Juana de la Cruz: Poems*, edited by Margaret Sayers Peden (Tempe, AZ: Bilingual Review Press, 1985).

160. More of Chiyō-ni's poetry can be found in *A History of Haiku, Volume 1*, by R. H. Blyth (Tokyo: The Hokuseido Press, 1963) and in *From the Country of Eight Islands*, translated and edited by Hiroaki Sato and Burton Watson (New York: Columbia University Press, 1986). I am grateful to Zen master Robert Aitken for sending me his translation and the D. T. Suzuki essay upon which I have drawn in the introduction; he has drawn on this material as well, in *A Zen Wave: Bashō's Haiku & Zen* (New York and Tokyo: Weatherhill, 1978).

164. Ann Griffiths's biography and a translation of her hymns and letters can be found in *Songs to Her God: Spirituality of Ann Griffiths* by A. M. Allchin (Cambridge, MA: Cowley Publications, 1987).

166. Emily Brontë's poetry can be found in *The Complete Poems* by Emily Brontë (New York and London: Penguin Books, 1993).

168. For more about Hayati and her poems, see *Sufi Women*, by Dr. Javad Nurbakhsh, translated by Leonard Lewisohn (New York: Khaniqahi-Nimatullahi Publications, 1983).

171. Emily Dickinson's poetry can be found in *The Complete Poems of Emily Dickinson*, edited by Thomas H. Johnson (Boston: Little Brown and Company, 1961). Many biographies and studies of her work are also available.

184. Other songs and accompanying music from St. Simon's Island can be found in *Slave Songs of the Georgia Sea Islands* by Lydia Parrish (New York: Creative Age Press, 1942).

186. Other songs and accompanying music collected by Eva A. Jessye are in *My Spirituals* by Eva A. Jessye (New York: Robbins-Engel, Inc., 1927).

188. For more of Christina Rossetti's poetry, see *The Complete Poems of Christina Rossetti*, a variorum edition in three volumes, edited and with textual notes and introductions by R. W. Crump (Baton Rouge and London: Louisiana State University Press, 1979, 1986, 1990).

193. Uvavnuk's story and song appear in Knud Rasmussen's *Report of the Fifth Thule Expedition, 1921–24*, Volume VII, no. 1, translated by W. Worster (Copenhagen: Gyldendalske Boghandel, Nordisk Forlag, 1929).

194. These two Kwakiutl prayers are adapted from texts in Franz Boas's *Religion of the Kwakiutl Indians* (New York: Columbia University Press, 1930).

196. For more about Owl Woman and her medicine songs, see *Papago Music*, by Frances Densmore, Bulletin 90, Bureau of American Ethnology, Washington, DC, 1929.

198. The Osage Woman's Initiation Song comes from *The Osage Tribe*, by Francis La Flesche, Volume I, 36th Annual Report, Bureau of American Ethnology, Washington, DC, 1921.

199. This version of the Shootingway ceremony comes from *Spider Woman: A Story of Navajo Weavers and Chanters*, by Gladys A. Reichard (Glorieta, NM: The Rio Grande Press, 1968). Many books exist about the Navajo Chantway material; one excellent one is *Beautyway: A Navajo Ceremonial*, by Leland Clifton Wyman, myth recorded and translated by Father Berard Haile (New York: Pantheon/Bollingen, 1957).

201. H.D.'s poetry is available in *Collected Poems 1912–1944*, edited by Louis L. Martz (New York: New Directions, 1983); *Trilogy*, by H.D. (New York: New Directions, 1973); *Hermetic Definition*, by H.D. (New York: New Directions, 1972); *et al.*

207. For more about Anna Akhmatova, see *The Complete Poems of Anna Akhmatova* (2 volumes), translated by Judith Hemschemeyer (Somerville, MA: Zephyr Press, 1990); *Poems of Akhmatova*, selected, translated, and introduced by Stanley Kunitz with Max Hayward (Boston and Toronto: Atlantic Monthly/ Little Brown, 1973); *Anna Akhmatova: Twenty Poems*, translated by Jane Kenyon (Saint Paul, MN: Eighties Press and Ally Press, 1985); and *Way of All Earth* by Anna Akhmatova, translated by D. M. Thomas (London: Martin Secker & Warburg Ltd., 1979).

211. Gabriela Mistral's poetry is available in *Selected Poems of Gabriela Mistral*,

translated by Langston Hughes (Bloomington: Indiana University Press, 1957); *Gabriela Mistral, A Reader*, translated by Maria Giachetti and edited by Marjorie Agosin (Fredonia, NY: White Pine Press, 1993); and *Selected Poems of Gabriela Mistral*, translated and edited by Doris Dana (Baltimore: The Johns Hopkins Press, 1971).

216. For more poems by Nelly Sachs, see *O The Chimneys: Selected Poems*, translated by Michael Hamburger, Christopher Holme, Ruth and Matthew Mead and Michael Roloff (New York: Farrar, Straus and Giroux, 1967) and *The Seeker*, translated by Ruth and Matthew Mead and Michael Hamburger (New York: Farrar, Straus and Giroux, 1970).

225. For more about Edith Södergran, see *Love & Solitude: Selected Poems, 1916–1923, Centennial Edition*, translated by Stina Katchadourian (Seattle: Fjord Press, 1992; PO Box 16349, Seattle WA 98116) and *Edith Södergran: Complete Poems*, translated by David McDuff (Newcastle upon Tyne, UK: Bloodaxe Books, 1984).

231. For more about Marina Tsvetaeva see *Selected Poems of Marina Tsvetayeva*, translated and introduced by Elaine Feinstein (New York: E. P. Dutton, 1986); *Selected Poems*, translated by David McDuff (Newcastle upon Tyne, UK: Bloodaxe Books, 1987); and *In the Inmost Hour of the Soul*, translated by Nina Kossman (Clifton, NJ: Humana Press, 1989). Some of her prose writings appear in *A Captive Spirit: Selected Prose*, translated and edited by J. Marin King (Ann Arbor: Ardis, 1980).

237. The translation of the poem by Kadya Molodowsky is from a book in progress, *Selected Poems of Kadya Molodowsky*, translated and with an introduction by Kathryn Hellerstein. Molodowsky's work also appears in several anthologies of women's poetry and Yiddish literature.

Acknowledgments

Many people have offered suggestions and support during the progress of this book. I would especially like to thank Stephen Mitchell, for whose 1989 anthology *The Enlightened Heart* the earliest of my translations in this book were made; his collection is the god-parent to this one and he has been generous throughout with suggestions and encouragement. Others for whose support and suggestions, early and late, I am grateful include Christopher Bamford, Stephen Barclay, Laura Fargas, Marjorie Fletcher, Sam Hamill, Andrew Harvey, Roald Hoffman, Mary Mackey, Dennis Maloney, Yvonne Rand, John Tarrant, Peter Turner, and Al Young. I thank Robert Aitken, Francisco X. Alarcón, Mariko Aratani, Coleman Barks, Robert Bly, Edwin A. Cranston, Paul Graves, Samuel Michael Halevi, Michael Hamburger, Thich Nhat Hanh, Linda Hess, Arnie Kotler, Julie Pickering, Liana Sakelliou, Miranda Shaw, Laura Anna Stortoni, Mu Ryang Sunim, and Mujin Sunim for their help in obtaining specific selections in this book.

I would also like to express my gratitude for the institutions in whose libraries I conducted my primary research: the collections and staff at the University of California at Berkeley, the Graduate Theological Union at Berkeley, the University of San Francisco, and the Mill Valley Public Library proved invaluable.

Lastly, I would like to thank Hugh Van Dusen, my HarperCollins editor, whose support brought this book into existence; David Bullen, for clothing its words in simplicity, elegance, and grace; and Michael Katz, for his heartful assistance, practical support, and guidance in every way beyond measure.

About the Editor

Jane Hirshfield is the author of three collections of poems, *The October Palace* (HarperCollins, 1994), *Of Gravity & Angels* (1988), and *Alaya* (1982). She is also editor and co-translator of *The Ink Dark Moon: Love Poems by Ono No Komachi and Izumi Shikibu, Women of the Ancient Court of Japan* (1990). Her poems have appeared in *The Atlantic, The Nation, The New Yorker, The American Poetry Review, Antaeus, Poetry, The Paris Review*, and many anthologies, and she has received a Guggenheim Fellowship, the Commonwealth Club of California's Poetry Medal, a Columbia University Translation Center Award, and other honors. A student of Zen since 1974, she lives in northern California.

Alphabetical Index of Authors

258